Park
Notes

An anthology
of writing and
art inspired by
a London park

SARAH PICKSTONE

DAUNT BOOKS

First published in Great Britain in 2014 by
Daunt Books
83 Marylebone High Street
London W1U 4QW

A CIP catalogue record for this title is available from
the British Library.

ISBN 978-1-907970-38-2

Designed by aka-alice.co.uk

Printed and bound by Graphicom, Vicenza, Italy

www.dauntbooks.co.uk

For Martin

Albie, Laurence and Elizabeth

Contents

Neo Classik, 2006

Preface

Sarah Pickstone

One weekday afternoon in October 2009, I was sitting on a plastic bag on the damp grass of Regents Park's Inner Circle, coffee in one hand, pencil in the other. I was trying to draw the sun – as it was lighting the noses and foreheads of park visitors staring out from the large windows of the café.

It is considered a bit unnecessary to draw outside these days, to see the world in texture, light and three dimensions. I like it. I like to draw connections between things; I like to draw a line along a page that connects the fronds of a willow to a neoclassical fountain from the 1950s, to a hijab, to a moth.

Along with the coffee that day, I had bought a yellow booklet – a story by Ali Smith, published by the Royal Parks. As the sun set and the noses and foreheads receded into the interior light of the café, I put pencil behind ear and began to read 'The Definite Article'.

There's a paragraph in Smith's story, where she recalls the writers who have once been connected to the park and as I read, I was reminded of the moment in *Middlemarch* – which George Eliot began writing while living in a villa just to the north of the park – where Dorothea is mesmerised, not by the classical statues of the museum but by a streak of sunlight falling across the floor. It occurred to me that my interest in drawing this park lay in a combination of nature and human narrative and that the park was in some way an exquisite example of this.

This moment marked the start of a new body of work for me. First I made a painting of Elizabeth Barrett Browning, stealing mistletoe from the park – you'll have to read 'The Definite Article' – and sent a jpeg to Ali Smith as a Christmas card. She came to the studio, liked it and bought it.

From there I read Virginia Woolf and drew her reading next to the lake, based on a photograph taken by her sister, Vanessa Bell. Sylvia Plath had lived close by and I tried to conjure her in the act of writing, perhaps looking at the same lake and seeing the reflected Hylas there. The lines of hair from Stevie Smith's drawing became part of my drawing of the *Willow*, and Katherine Mansfield (who was sent to school nearby from distant Wellington and whose transformative stories I loved) took on the mantle of the moth. Angela Carter, although a devoted South Londoner, gave her twins from *Wise Children* their only north London outing to this park and they turned up in my painting of the fountain of Triton.

These paintings and several more made up The Writers Series, which was exhibited at the New Art Centre, Roche Court, in 2013. Marina Warner's essay here served as an introduction to that show.

The park has always held a symbolic meaning for me. I'm drawn to the idea of a place, full of connections and pathways and the potential for play. In so many ways the park is a metaphor for painting itself.

So *Park Notes* was born in the heart of London. Above all it is a book about the process of making work. It is an eclectic compilation that pays homage to the sources of The Writers Series and expands to include contemporary work by today's writers. Iain Sinclair relates his walks with photographer Stephen Gill, Craig Taylor gives us the story of his guide Gordon, and Amanda Coe writes about her family's dog with an eye to Flush (Elizabeth Barrett's spaniel, eponymous hero of Woolf's short novella). Fiona Banner's *Full Stop* sculptures serve here to remind me of the value of structure and the importance of the mind's eye. For a transatlantic view, I include Patti Smith, who followed Rimbaud here and who lends us a Polaroid: a leaf, a blood stain, an image of ink and mortality. Each has a connection – through either work, biography or imagination – to the park, and *Park Notes* opens up a dialogue between artists, writers and regular park dwellers by bringing these paintings and writings together. The park is a source and a symbol for communal creativity. Like a series of strangers walking pathways that interconnect, art too comes out of one thing and into another, as sure as the seasons.

3

Fiona Banner, *Playbill, Broadway and Futura*, 2002. Full Stops: steel, paint.

Park 2, 2004

Elizabeth Barrett Browning Steals Mistletoe, 2010

The Definite Article
Ali Smith

I stepped out of the city and into the park. It was as simple as that.

It was January, it was a foggy day in London town, I had got off the tube at Great Portland Street and come up and out into the dark of the day, I was on my way to an urgent meeting about funding. It was possible in the current climate that funding was going to be withdrawn so we were having to have an urgent meeting urgently to decide on the right kind of rhetoric. This would ensure the right developmental strategy which would in turn ensure that funding wouldn't conclude in this way at this time. I had come the whole way underground saying over and over in my head, urgent, ensure, feasibility, margin, assessment, management, rationalisation, developmental strategy, strategic development, current climate, project incentive, core values, shouldn't conclude, in this way, at this time. But it also had to be unthreatening, the language we were to use to ensure etc, so I went up the stairs repeating to myself the phrase not a problem not a problem not a problem, then stopped for a moment at the Tube exit because (ow) my eye was really hurting, out of nowhere I'd got something in my eye.

It made everything else disappear. I stopped and stood. I blinked. I felt about in one of my pockets, folded the edge of a Kleenex into what felt like a point and ran it along the inside of my lower lid. I blinked again and looked to see. The something that had been in my eye was stuck now on the edge of the Kleenex. It was tiny, and it might once have had legs, hard to tell now. Maybe its legs were still in my eye; the eye was still stinging a little, still running. Running. Legs. Ha ha.

Urgent. Core values. Shouldn't conclude. The eye was still a bit sore. I tried focussing into the distance. What I saw was the edge of the park. Then I saw myself pressing the button on the pedestrian crossing. Then I was crossing the road anyway, between the fast-coming cars, before I changed my mind.

7

On the wide path on Avenue Gardens I dried a bit of bench with the Kleenex I still had in my hand. I sat down and held my other hand over the sore eye. I could hear traffic, background, faded. When my eye stopped stinging, I'd go back.

But it was turning into one of the days in January that spring sends ahead of itself. The fog would burn off. It was burning off right now. It was clearing, I could see. There were magpies. There were pigeons. There were all sorts of birds, everywhere. When was the last time I had looked at a blackbird, or at a robin? When was the last time I had looked properly at anything? There were runners on the park's paths. There was a cordon of very young schoolchildren out on a trip in the middle of the day. There was a man whistling, walking along holding a can of Skol ahead of himself. He was holding the can like a compass. There was a man in a wheelchair, being wheeled by a boy. The boy looked very like him. There was a man with a camera on a tripod. He was filming a woman who'd stopped to feed a squirrel. There was a woman doing a sideways stepping walking exercise. There were two joggers and a dog. The dog, keeping the pace beside them, looked full of happiness, and there were patterns everywhere, in the line of benches stretching towards and away from me, in the fountains and the stone urns, in the trees, in the died-back tidied beds of flowers, and that's when I remembered out of nowhere something I hadn't thought about in years, it's back when I'm twenty-five, we've been together for six weeks, we've no money, it's my birthday and as a birthday present you sit me down and blindfold me. You lead me by the hand, blindfolded, out of the flat to where your old Mini with the holes in its floor is parked. You guide me into the car and then you drive me I have no idea where. There's a strangeness in every noise. Everything I touch and everything that touches me is so complex that all my senses flare. How closed-in things are when we're in the car, and is this what open actually means, when you get me out of it, still blindfolded, and lead me up a steep path, into what feels like somewhere whose openness will never end? At the top of this steepness we stop. You take me by the shoulders and turn me so that I'm facing something I can't see yet. You wish me happy birthday. Then you take the blind-fold off me.

It's light, colour, it's the top of the hill. It's the city itself I see under the huge sky. It was one of the best birthday presents I'd ever been given, I knew now so many birthdays on, twenty-five years later, a different person yet the same person, sitting in the park in the future, one hand over one eye. Where were you now? I wondered. What were you doing right now in the world?

A bee passed me. It was quite a large bee, bright yellow and black. A bee in January? Far too early in the year for a bee to be out, it should be wintering, it would surely die. I'd better go, I thought. I had a (not a problem) meeting to chair, and as clear as day the thought came into my head. I could follow that bee up Avenue Gardens. I could turn left and go to the Rose Garden. I hadn't been to the Rose Garden for years. There'd surely be some roses out, regardless of January, and I could go and see the little statue of Cupid with his arrows, was I remembering rightly, riding on the back of a stone duck or a goose or something? Cupid, with the tips of his arrows dipped in honey. And what was that old

poem, about Cupid getting stung by a bee and complaining to his mother, Venus, and her holding her sides laughing at him because of the stings his arrows give lovers, and him put out by a tiny bee? Cupid, in a bed of roses, no, Cupid, as he lay among, Roses by a bee got stung. It was years since I'd thought of that poem.

It was years since I'd thought about any poem.

I would go and look at the little statue to see if Cupid really was sitting on the back of a bird, or if I was just imagining it. When I'd done that I could go to the meeting.

Urgent. The word was a bit shaming when I thought about it. Not a problem. What did not a problem actually mean?

I would go to the Rose Garden. From there I would walk to the boating lake; then up past the sports pitches to the big fountain, and round by the zoo.

From there I'd go to the bot-tom of Primrose Hill, choose a path, any path, and follow it to the top.

That was all, the passing thought, the mere slant of the thought of all the different possible ways there are just to cross a park, and that did it, the morning shook its pelt, slipped its rein and did a sideways dash across Regent's Park – no, not just Regent's Park but *the* Regent's Park, *the* park, the definite article, the park that began as a forest whose sky was the tops of its trees, then the park of the left-handed King on horseback chasing the stag (and that's why the park is the lopsided shape it is, because Henry the Eighth was left-handed, so when he drew over the map of the Abbess's woods to mark the land he wanted *thus*, that's what his hand did, made a great curve there and a straight line there). The park of grazing smutty sheep (it's Henry James who called them smutty), the park of visions and assignations, fairs and ballads, footpads in their element, prostitutes in their ribbons. The park of the pretty girl out walking among the pretty flowers, taken suddenly and kissed hard on the mouth, *pray, alarm yourself not, Madame, you can now boast you've been kissed by Dick Turpin*. The park with the roofless theatre, *A Midsummer Night's Dream* in the midsummer air. The park where the crowds fed as much cake and biscuit as they could to Jumbo, The Biggest Elephant In The World, who'd been sold to America, in the hope it'd make him too heavy to be shipped across the Atlantic.

First it was Cromwell felling the trees for the Navy, *534 acres with 124 deer and 16,297 trees of oak, ash, elm, white thorn and maple*. Then it was Nash, deciding what new trees to use, pairing the colours of different kinds of tree to suit his villas. Then they felled the trees all over again for the twentieth century wars. More than three hundred bombs changed the shape of the place in the 1940s. And now it's now. The park that began with the lords and the ladies in their carriages. The park that evolved, that learned to open its gates to everybody, to hold all the city's hundreds of languages, the city's efflorescence, in the one place. *Great forest of wooded glades*; the first written description we have of the Forest of Middlesex, which became the Great Chase, the Marrowbone, the Marybone, the Marylebone Pleasure Gardens, the Marylebone Park, the Regent's Park, where today, like any old day of the week, the day in the park curved itself off like a bird into the air over the seven thousand five hundred trees, the

Willow, 2011

laughable colours of duck, the black swans in the Rose Garden drinking the earlier drizzle off their own backs, all the people on their way to work who love to walk through the park, the young couple slowing their pace for their old slow dog on the Broad Walk, the man shouting at the woman cyclist and the cyclist giving him the perfectly reversed V sign over her shoulder, the magpies gathering in wait for feeding time over the zoo's walls, the Primrose Hill bookshop where stray leaves from the park blow in at the door all year round.

The day in the park, like any old day, took its usual bee-line, one never threatened by mere winter (which only makes the fountains more beautiful, the ice forming all down the sides of them), and one that always makes something of itself, like the honey the Regent's Park bees make of their visits to the lime trees in Avenue Gardens; or the honey that tastes of roses in the seasons when the Rose Garden proves good pickings for the bees. Amber Queen. English Miss. Wandering Minstrel. Sweet Dreams. Ingrid Bergman. Anna Ford. Mayor of Casterbridge. Old Yellow Scotch. There are hives all over the park where, right now, the bees would be crowding together to keep the temperature up, would be taking turns to be circled and warmed by all the other bees, would be tending to the year's future bees in their cells; there are beehives in good quiet places all over the park.

Look at that, nothing but a passing honeybee, the kind of nothing that has two sets of eyes, that makes a thousand flower-visits a day, a creature so clever that bees are already teaching themselves to combat the mites and diseases that have been killing them off so rapidly and so mysteriously (to humans at least) over the past few years. What's honey? A sweetener? Two pounds of honey equals a hundred thousand bee miles. The ancient Egyptians were the first to use it as an antiseptic, it's good on a burn, and it's not just good with a cough or a sore throat, it can help fight anthrax, diphtheria, cholera, MRSA, and when doctors transplant people's corneas the replacements are transported in honey.

Without bees? Nothing. Nothing pollinated. Hardly any fruit, almost no vegetables. All the food chains disrupted, from the human one down to the insect.

The beekeeper's got twenty-eight hives in the park at the moment. He has no idea if they'll survive the winter. Last year in the park only five out of twenty colonies survived, and the year that followed was rough; a too-warm February, a too-cold spring, a too-wet summer; the bees needed supplementary feeding, and God knows what's to come. He began with imported New Zealand queens; they're pretty, bright yellow and black. He's worked at creating new colonies, new queens, in case of the same kind of bee loss as last year.

Urgent. Current climate. He works for no salary. You might say it's a labour of love. He makes a tiny profit on the honey he sells. Local feral bees are much blacker in colour. Last year he saw the yellow of the bees foraging in the roses by the cafe in the Inner Circle and he knew immediately they were Regent's Park's bees. The summer honey tasted, last year, of lime and somehow of passionfruit. Does light have a taste? Does the park have a taste? The late extraction honey last year was sweet, dark and powerful.

Could any place be more historied and less ghostly? Where's the ghost of the poet, Elizabeth Barrett, stealing the park's flowers to put in an envelope addressed to her fiancé, Robert, in Italy? Where are the ghosts of Percy Bysshe Shelley and Mary Shelley, sailing their paper boats on the pond? Where are the ghosts of the forty-odd people who went skating in January in 1867 and drowned in the lake when the ice gave way? Even them, cold and shivering, with the right to be a bit aggrieved, the right to hang about complaining for over a century, they're just not here. It's all open air. There's nothing dead and gone about it. Elizabeth Bowen, watching the swans in their *slow indignation* and Richard Wagner standing at the lake throwing bread to the ducks; and Samuel Johnson causing a mini riot because it's too wet for the fireworks he's come to see; Charles Dickens, melancholy, a woman's been drowned in the canal; old George Bernard Shaw young again on the seat of a far-too-fast bike; Dodie Smith filling the park with the imaginary barks of dogs; Sylvia Plath, real as can be, hearing the hungry lion roar over the

13

crib of her newborn child; then Ted Hughes, newly bereaved, the zoo-wolf howl in his ears; and Virginia Woolf herself, howling or furious or sad, doesn't matter which, walking and walking by the flower-beds till it cheers her up, leaves her happily *making up phrases.*

There's the woman who comes into the park at half past six in the morning and spends all the daylight hours leaving little mounds of cake and sunflower seeds (she always buys organic), in the same places so the wild-life will find it there when it comes looking.

There's the story of the man who, nearly two hundred years ago, bought four tiny birds from a sailor he met in the park. He put the birds in his pocket. When he got back to his lodgings he set the birds free. He watched them soar up over London.

Bet you any money, even if they'd been snared there in the first place, those birds flew straight back to the park.

'One entire Park, compleat in unity of character'. Endless stories, all crossing across each other, and mine tiny, negligent, quick as a blink, where nothing much happened except this:

I stepped out of myself and into the park, I stepped off the pavement and into a place where there's never a conclusion, where regardless of wars, tragedies, losses, finds, the sting or the sweetness of what's gone in a life, or the preoccupations of any single time, any single being, on it goes, the open-air theatre of flowers, trees, birds, bees, the open vision at the heart of the old city.

In this way, at this time, nothing concluded.

In other words: in foggy London town the sun, shining everywhere. The meeting could wait. It did wait, while I sat on the bench in Avenue Gardens and thought about the poem where the god of love gets stung by a bee and his mother laughs at him, and about whether there were as many different kinds of rose in the Rose Garden as there were different languages spoken in the city of London, and about the day back then when a visit to the park gave me back my own senses.

I had no idea where you were today in the world. But I remem-bered, sitting there in the park, what it meant that our paths had crossed. I remembered, too, that old Mini you had and how its floor had rusted right through, and how we could look down and see the surface of the road pass so quickly beneath us that going at thirty miles per hour, twenty, ten, even something near walking-pace, pierced me every time with what it was that words like fast or slow or road or city meant.

Urgent. Core values.

When I got cold I walked across the park in the happy noise of blackbirds.

Then I went to the top of the hill and looked at the view. The city gathered round the park and rose out of itself as usual. I saw it all over again, as if for the first time.

15

Bed, 2004

Stevie Smith and the Willow, 2011

Stevie Smith and the Willow
Paul Hobson

A common method of exploring a subject's interior world is to ask them to imagine a space – a garden, a room, a stage – that can be populated by them, when prompted, with imaginary objects or scenarios that will illuminate their psychological situation. Language triggers images instantly, and we know that space is a necessary condition for the imagination since, if an image is a visual thought, it requires the virtual space in which to exist. For Sarah Pickstone, it is an imaginary park that has for some years provided the metaphorical space for her interrogation of the elusive and fugitive nature of image-making and its relationship to language and inter-subjective expression.

Inspired by the history and physical features of Regent's Park in London, Pickstone brings herself into communion with the iconic female writers who visited the park in the twentieth century. Known as The Writers Series, this group of paintings evokes the influence of memory, imagination and the natural landscape on writers such as Katherine Mansfield, Sylvia Plath, Virginia Woolf and others. As with Modernist literature, all the paintings in the series allow psychological, historical and geographical space to flow into one another, creating the sense that the world in the painting lies somewhere between our physical and more essential interior world.

To accompany her famous poem 'Not Waving but Drowning', British poet and novelist Stevie Smith scribbled a drawing of a girl submerged to her waist in water. Pickstone's enigmatic painting *Stevie Smith and the Willow* (which won the prestigious John Moores Painting Prize in 2012) re-locates the girl beneath a specific willow tree in Regent's Park. The tree is rendered in three torrential bands of triangulated yellow, green and brown. Elsewhere the palette is limited, with the tree trunk, central figure and reflections in the water in uniform grey washes. The painting is large, and the white ground gives the work a flatness that is reinforced by the angularity of the foliage and the doodle-like central character. The work combines a strong painterly quality with a digital aesthetic, as if the image has been created on the blank screen of a tablet, quickly sketched in parts and embellished with texture elsewhere. What is striking about the painting is its uncanny sense of time – not so much a lived moment caught in suspension as a screen-grab of an image experienced time and time again. The overall effect is hybrid and strangely alienating.

All of this, of course, is testimony to the artist's ability to translate into a pictorial scheme her version of the psycho-geography and artistic temperament of Stevie Smith and the poem for which she is best known.

Smith's much-loved poem 'Not Waving but Drowning' of 1957 addresses the theme of isolation in a world of interaction; how signs, gestures and images can be – and often are – misinterpreted; how most of us exist within ourselves without a clear sense of authorship, unable to fully recognise the intentions of others. Conventional language and behaviour emerge as approximate and haphazard modes of self-expression, exposing the unbridgeable void between the private and the public.

This was, we know, how Stevie Smith experienced the world. Smith was a writer of intense shyness and rare sensitivity who suffered from depression all her life and often felt an acute sense of isolation from those around her. She once said that 'being alive is like being in enemy territory'. Diagnosed with tuberculosis at the age of five, and in and out of sanatoria for years, Smith developing a life-long obsession with death, which is a recurring theme in her work. The poet openly admitted that 'my poems are a bit deathwards in their wish'. As an extension of Smith's preoccupation with the morbid, her poetry often deals with the sinister reality that lurks behind appealing or innocent appearances, while often referencing the cadence of nursery rhymes. Smith drew small pictures to accompany many of her poems, which made it more difficult to find publishers at the time. Like the poems themselves, the pictures are both charming and unsettling in their effect.

Fortunately, the poet did not pursue the attractions of death, however much she might have thought of it. She evidently found that she could cope with alien territory by living, as she put it, 'on the edge' and in the 'merciful house' that held the 'guardian Lion' she also knew as her aunt, with whom she had gone to live in Palmers Green in North London following her mother's death in 1918. However, as for many of the Modernist writers with whom she shares company in The Writers Series, she struggled against the lure of death and suicide, fighting battles through which existence and subjectivity became acutely understood.

Pickstone's idea of the park is of a constructed social space where people come together, achieve a conventional proximity but retain a fundamental isolation. It provides a useful metaphorical space for her reverie on Stevie Smith's poetic legacy and that of the other iconic feminist writers to whom she is drawn. Although a simple idea and device, her park is best described as an abstraction, more like a mood or feeling: an imaginary space that might reveal something about our self. It is fictional, but perhaps when Stevie Smith talks of a life lived in 'enemy territory' she is recognising that we are always more fully and clearly realised as works of fiction in the imaginations of others.

19

Stevie Smith and the Willow, detail, 2011

Love is Everything, One Looks for It, 2013

Not *Waving but Drowning*

NOBODY heard him, the dead man,
But still he lay moaning:
I was much further out than you thought
And not waving but drowning.

Poor chap, he always loved larking
And now he's dead
It must have been too cold for him his heart
They said.   [gave way,

Oh, no no no, it was too cold always
(Still the dead one lay moaning)
I was much too far out all my life
And not waving but drowning.

[13]

Stevie Smith, 'Not Waving but Drowning', 1957

Sylvia, 2010

Sylvia Plath

'On the Difficulty of Conjuring Up a Dryad' *Sylvia Plath*

Ravening through the persistent bric-à-brac
Of blunt pencils, rose-sprigged coffee cup,
Postage stamps, stacked books' clamor and yawp,
Neighborhood cockcrow – all nature's prodigal
$\qquad\qquad\qquad\qquad\qquad$ backtalk,
$\qquad$ The vaunting mind
$\qquad$ Snubs impromptu spiels of wind
$\qquad$ And wrestles to impose
$\qquad$ Its own order on what is.

'With my fantasy alone,' brags the importunate head,
Arrogant among rook-tongued spaces
Sheep greens, finned falls, 'I shall compose a crisis
To stun sky black out, drive gibbering mad
$\qquad$ Trout, cock, ram,
$\qquad$ That bulk so calm
$\qquad$ On my jealous stare,
$\qquad$ Self-sufficient as they are.'

But no hocus-pocus of green angels
Damasks with dazzle the threadbare eye;
'My trouble, doctor, is: I see a tree,
And that damn scrupulous tree won't practice wiles
$\qquad$ To beguile sight:
$\qquad$ E.g., by cant of light
$\qquad$ Concoct a Daphne;
$\qquad$ My tree stays tree.

'However I wrench obstinate bark and trunk
To my sweet will, no luminous shape

Steps out radiant in limb, eye, lip,
To hoodwink the honest earth which pointblank
    Spurns such fiction
    As nymphs; cold vision
    Will have no counterfeit
    Palmed off on it.

'No doubt now in dream-propertied fall
                    some moon-eyed,
Star-lucky sleight-of-hand man watches
My jilting lady squander coin, gold leaf stock ditches,
And the opulent air go studded with seed,
    While this beggared brain
    Hatches no fortune,
    But from the leaf, from grass,
    Thieves what it has.'

Drawing by Sylvia Plath, *Willow near Grantchester*

Sylvia Googled, 2010

Plath Winged, 2010

Sylvia Plath interviewing Elizabeth Bowen for *Mademoiselle*, May 1953

Elizabeth Bowen

From
Tears, Idle Tears
Elizabeth Bowen

Frederick burst into tears in the middle of Regent's Park. His mother, seeing what was about to happen, had cried: 'Frederick, you *can't* – in the middle of Regent's Park!' Really, this was a corner, one of those lively corners just inside a big gate, where two walks meet and a bridge starts across the pretty, winding lake. People were passing quickly; the bridge rang with feet. Poplars stood up like delicate green brooms; diaphanous willows whose weeping was not shocking quivered over the lake. May sun spattered gold through the breezy trees; the tulips though falling open were still gay; three girls ina long boat shot under the bridge. Frederick, knees trembling, butted towards his mother, a crimson convulsed face, as though he had the idea of burying himself in her. She whipped out a handkerchief and dabbed at him with it under his grey felt hat, exclaiming meanwhile in fearful mortification: 'You really haven't got to be such a *baby*!' Her tone attracted the notice of several people, who might otherwise have thought he was having something taken out of his eye.

He was too big to cry: the whole scene was disgraceful. He wore a grey flannel knickerbocker suit and looked like a schoolboy; though in fact he was seven, still doing lessons at home. His mother said to him almost every week: 'I don't know what they will think when you go to school!' His tears were a shame of which she could speak to no one; no offensive weakness of body could have upset her more. Once she had got so far as taking her pen up to write to the Mother's Advice column of a helpful woman's weekly about them. She began: 'I am a widow; young, good tempered, and my friends all tell me that I have great control. But my little boy—' She intended to sign herself 'Mrs D., Surrey'. But then she had stopped and thought no, no: after all, he is Toppy's son... She was a gallant-looking, correct woman, wearing today in London a coat and skirt, a silver fox, white gloves and a dark-blue toque put on exactly right – not the sort of woman you ought to see in a Park with a great blubbering boy belonging to her. She looked a mother of sons, but not of a son of this kind, and should more properly, really, have been walking a dog. 'Come on!' she said, as though the bridge, the poplars, the people staring were to be borne no longer. She began to walk on quickly, along the edge of the lake, parallel with the park's girdle of trees and the dark, haughty windows of Cornwall Terrace looking at her over the red may. They had meant to go to the Zoo, but now she had changed her mind: Frederick did not deserve the Zoo.

Frederick stumbled along beside her, too miserable to notice. His mother seldom openly punished him, but often revenged herself on him in small ways. He could feel how just this was. His own incontinence in the matter of tears was as shocking to him, as bowing-down, as annulling, as it could be to her. He never knew what happened – a cold, black pit with no bottom opened inside himself; a red-hot bellwire jagged up through him from the pit of his frozen belly to the caves of his eyes. Then the hot, gummy rush of tears, the convulsion of his features, the terrible, square grin he felt his mouth take all made him his own shameful and squalid enemy. Despair howled round his inside like a wind, and through his streaming eyes he saw everything quake. Anyone's being there – and most of all his mother – drove this catastrophe on him. He never cried like this when he was alone.

Bowen Smokes, 2010

Elizabeth Bowen in Regent's Park
Lara Feigel

In 1935 the Anglo-Irish novelist Elizabeth Bowen and her husband Alan Cameron leased a flat in one of the white Regency terraces overlooking Regent's Park. Bowen told Virginia Woolf that the flat at Number 2 Clarence Terrace was 'very lovely with green reflections inside from the trees such as I have only seen otherwise in a country house'. The ceilings were high and the windows wide; there was a balcony, from which she could survey the boating lake on the west side of the park. For the next fifteen years this became Bowen's personal landscape. Looking out from her balcony and wandering around the lake or through the rose garden, she watched as one season gave way to another and as peace gave way to war.

Bowen later wrote that the immediate appeal of Regent's Park was its literary quality. Even after she had moved there, it seemed like something out of a book. Commissioned to write a piece about her local area, she described the 'infinitely romantic mystery' of the vistas of water

and trees by the boating lake and reflected that 'the swaggering, lyrical imperfection of Regent's Park' with its combination of audacious Nash villas and natural loveliness seemed to correspond with 'something in the creative nature'. Bowen thought that this accounted for why so many artists had chosen to make it their home. Certainly, the park joined her ancestral Irish home, Bowen's Court, as one of the two central settings of her own fiction.

If Bowen was a novelist of place, then her places were always imbued with a psychological charge. This was why the landscapes surrounding her own homes were so important for her; they had witnessed and inflected her internal psychological states. The two novels that Bowen wrote after moving to Clarence Terrace both open in Regent's Park. *The Death of the Heart* (1938) begins in a 1930s winter; there is ice floating on the lake; swans swim 'in slow indignation' in the remaining channels. The 'pallid withdrawn Regency terraces' are imbued with 'an unnatural burnish' as though cold has transmuted into light.

The Heat of the Day (1948) opens in the early evening of the first Sunday of September, 1942. There is an orchestra playing in the open-air theatre where the first fallen leaves of autumn drift onto the grass stage. As evening comes, the turquoise afternoon sky gains transparency; each leaf is defined in the 'glass-clear darkness' forming in the thicket behind the orchestra.

By the time Bowen came to write *The Heat of the Day*, both the park that she loved and her own terrace had been damaged by war. The park had also become the setting for the love affair that was both the most intensely happy and the most anguished experience of her life.

Only five days into the Blitz, on 12 September 1940, Clarence Terrace was shut after a bomb fell in the street. When Bowen returned two weeks later, there were still barriers and bomb-notices at every entrance. 'Through the railings I watch dahlias blaze out their colour,' she wrote in an article. 'Leaves fill the empty deck-chairs; in the sunshine water-fowl, used to so much attention, mope round the unpeopled rim of the lake.' Bowen reported to her cousin in neutral Ireland that Clarence Terrace looked 'like a street in a city of the dead, with dead leaves and bits of paper blowing about'. Going to bed, she felt as if she was sleeping in the corner of a deserted palace. She only left the house to buy loaves and bottles of milk, largely to feed Lawrence the cat.

It was a few months after this that Bowen met Charles Ritchie, a Canadian diplomat stationed in London. He was six years younger than her; intelligent, irresponsible, fickle and unprepared to fall precipitously and irrevocably in love with a woman whom at first glance he described as 'well-dressed middle-aged with the air of being the somewhat worldly wife of a don'. From the start, this was a love affair powered by Bowen, whose faith in Ritchie was unassailable and whose capacity for love was immense. But if Ritchie was less prepared for love than Bowen, he was quickly swept into a romance that gained its charge from the fairy-tale atmosphere of Regent's Park.

Dreamlike days were spent watching the swans go by on

33

the river or lying talking on the grass. In early September, on one of the last, borrowed days of summer, they visited the rose garden. This was an afternoon that both would later see as marking the blooming of their happiness. Recording it in his diary, Ritchie described how he had seen the flowers through the lens of his lover's sensibility:

> The whole scene, the misty river, the Regency villas with their walled gardens and damp lawns, and the late September afternoon weather blended into a dream – a dream in which these were all symbols soaked with a mysterious associative power – Regent's Park – a landscape of love. A black swan floating downstream in the evening light – the dark purplish-red roses whose petals already lay scattered – the deserted Nash house with its flaking stucco colonnade and overgrown gardens – all were symbols speaking a language which by some miracle we could understand together.

If Regent's Park was a landscape of love, then it was a landscape fashioned by Bowen, through her novels and through

her gift for living in the present, turning afternoons in the park into perfect moments outside time. Her capacity for intensely inhabiting the present had been sharpened by war, when lovers throughout London were aware that any moment could be their last. It is a love memorialised in *The Heat of the Day* where Bowen describes the 'great globular roses, today at the height of their second blooming' that burn more fiercely as the sun descends, dazzling the lake. This opening scene is all the more potent because the September dusk occurs in wartime; the falling leaves are described as 'crepitating as though in the act of dying'.

In 1951 Bowen gave up the flat in Clarence Terrace. The park did not feature in any subsequent novels and she did not revisit it with Charles Ritchie after the war, when they tended to meet in Ireland or abroad. Gradually the relationship became more one-sided as Ritchie attempted to escape Bowen's exacting hold over him. But both continued to memorialise the park as the setting for an unreal but idyllic era of mutual love. In 1950 Bowen wrote to Ritchie regretting that they had not found the time to walk there together on his last visit to London:

A particular gentle tract of our happiness belongs to it – walks after lunch, walks when we were coming back here to this house for tea. So much so that the park has become you for me.

After Bowen's death in 1973, Ritchie visited the park again. It was too early for the full explosion of roses, but the park was still exactly as he remembered it. And he found that wandering around the lake and surveying the rose garden both simplified and intensified his grief:

I shall never see her again in this world or the next … She will never advance to me across the grass of Regent's Park at any time of day. She is gone from me forever.

35

Plane, 2011

Night Moths
Jackie Kay

Last night when I opened my back door
Ten red moths flew into my kitchen,
Their red and black paper wings, delicate as lanterns,
At night they came to light like motifs of folklore.
And now, suddenly ten, lined across my wall –
And kept so still – I wondered if they were ill.

I captured each visitor, in an empty glass
– The ancestors come in many guises –
And took each one to the open door, so soon,
And watched, as under the light of the one winged moon
Over the fence and into the starry sky,
The fluttering wings became a hello and goodbye.

Katherine Mansfield's Moth, 2011

Red Underwing, 2010

From
Notebooks
Katherine Mansfield

Notebook 16, May 21, 1919:

The red geraniums have bought the garden over
my head. They are there established, back in the
old home, every leaf and flower unpacked and in its
place – and quite determined that no power on earth
will ever move them again. Well, *that* I don't mind.
But why should they make me feel a stranger? Why
should they ask me every time I go near: 'And what
are *you* doing in a London garden?' They burn with
arrogance & pride. And I am the little colonial walking in the London garden path – allowed to look,
perhaps, but not to linger. If I lie on the grass they
positively shout at me. Look at her lying on *our* grass,
pretending she lives here, pretending this is her garden & that tall back on the house with the windows
open & the coloured curtains lifting is her house. She
is a stranger – an alien. She is nothing but a little girl
sitting on the Tinakori hills & dreaming: I went to
London and married an Englishman & we lived in a
tall grave house with red geraniums & white daisies
in the garden at the back. *Im*–prudence!

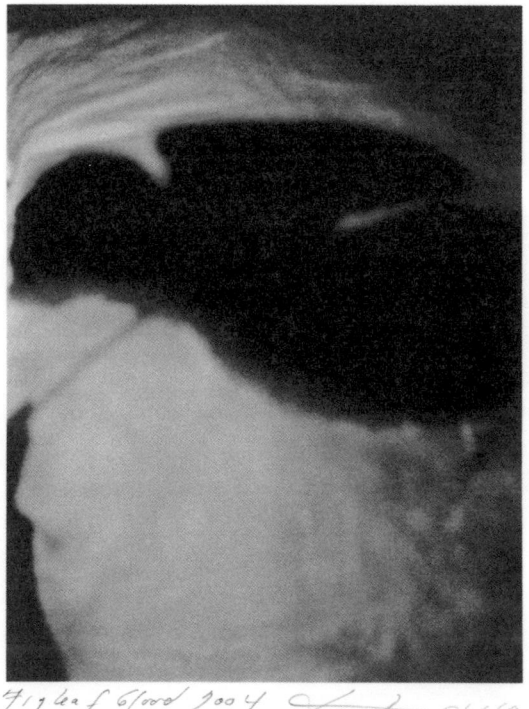

Patti Smith, *Fig leaf blood*, 2004

I wonder why it should be so difficult to be humble.
I do not think I am a good writer; I realise my faults
better than anyone else could realise them. I know
exactly where I fail. And yet, when I have finished a
story & before I have begun another I catch myself
preening my feathers. It is disheartening. There
seems to be some bad old pride in my heart; a root
of it that puts out a thick shoot on the slightest prov-
ocation . . . this interferes very much with work. One
can't be calm, clear, good as one must be while it
goes on. I look at the mountains, I try to pray, &
think of something *clever*. It's a kind of excitement
within one which shouldn't be there. Calm yourself.
Clear yourself. And anything that I write in this
mood will be no good; it will be full of *sediment*. If
I were well I would go off by myself somewhere &
sit under a tree. Once must learn, one must practise
to *forget* oneself. I can't tell the truth about Aunt
Anne unless I am free to enter into her life without self-consciousness. Oh God! I am divided still.
I am bad. I fail in my personal life. I lapse into
impatience, temper, vanity & so I fail as they priest.
Perhaps poetry will help.

I have just thoroughly cleaned & attended to
my fountain pen. If after this it leaks then it is
no gentleman!

Mansfield Googled, 2011

Woolf, 2010

Virginia Woolf

The Death Of The Moth
Virginia Woolf

Moths that fly by day are not properly to be called moths; they do not excite that pleasant sense of dark autumn nights and ivy-blossom which the commonest yellow-underwing asleep in the shadow of the curtain never fails to rouse in us. They are hybrid creatures, neither gay like butterflies nor sombre like their own species. Nevertheless the present specimen, with his narrow hay-coloured wings, fringed with a tassel of the same colour, seemed to be content with life. It was a pleasant morning, mid-September, mild, benignant, yet with a keener breath than that of the summer months. The plough was already scoring the field opposite the window, and where the share had been, the earth was pressed flat and gleamed with moisture. Such vigour came rolling in from the fields and the down beyond that it was difficult to keep the eyes strictly turned upon the book. The rooks too were keeping one of their annual festivities; soaring round the tree tops until it looked as if a vast net with thousands of black knots in it had been cast up into the air; which, after a few moments sank slowly down upon the trees until every twig seemed to have a knot at the end of it. Then, suddenly, the net would be thrown into the air again in a wider circle this time, with the utmost clamour and vociferation, as though to be thrown into the air and settle slowly down upon the tree tops were a tremendously exciting experience.

The same energy which inspired the rooks, the ploughmen, the horses, and even, it seemed, the lean bare-backed downs, sent the moth fluttering from side to side of his square of the windowpane. One could not help watching him. One, was, indeed, conscious of a queer feeling of pity for him. The possibilities of pleasure seemed that morning so enormous and so various that to have only a moth's part in life, and a day moth's at that, appeared a hard fate, and his zest in enjoying his meagre opportunities to the full, pathetic. He flew vigorously to one corner of his compartment, and, after waiting there a second, flew across to the other. What remained for him

The Death of the Moth, Virginia Woolf, cover by Vanessa Bell, 1942

but to fly to a third corner and then to a fourth? That was all he could do, in spite of the size of the downs, the width of the sky, the far-off smoke of houses, and the romantic voice, now and then, of a steamer out at sea. What he could do he did. Watching him, it seemed as if a fibre, very thin but pure, of the enormous energy of the world had been thrust into his frail and diminutive body. As often as he crossed the pane, I could fancy that a thread of vital light became visible. He was little or nothing but life.

Yet, because he was so small, and so simple a form of the energy that was rolling in at the open window and driving its way through so many narrow and intricate corridors in my own brain and in those of other human beings, there was something marvellous as well as pathetic about him. It was as if someone had taken a tiny bead of pure life and decking it as lightly as possible with down and feathers, had set it dancing and zigzagging to show us the true nature of life. Thus displayed one could not get over the strangeness of it. One is apt to forget all about life, seeing it humped and bossed and garnished and cumbered so that it has to move with the greatest circumspection and dignity. Again, the thought of all that life might have been had he been born in any other shape caused one to view his simple activities with a kind of pity.

After a time, tired by his dancing apparently, he settled on the window ledge in the sun, and, the queer spectacle being at an end, I forgot about him. Then, looking up, my eye was caught by him. He was trying to resume his dancing, but seemed either so stiff or so awkward that he could only flutter to the bottom of the windowpane; and when he tried to fly across it he failed. Being intent on other matters I watched these futile attempts for a time without thinking, unconsciously waiting for him to

47

resume his flight, as one waits for a machine, that has stopped momentarily, to start again without considering the reason of its failure. After perhaps a seventh attempt he slipped from the wooden ledge and fell, fluttering his wings, on to his back on the windowsill. The helplessness of his attitude roused me. It flashed upon me that he was in difficulties; he could no longer raise himself; his legs struggled vainly. But, as I stretched out a pencil, meaning to help him to right himself, it came over me that the failure and awkwardness were the approach of death. I laid the pencil down again.

The legs agitated themselves once more. I looked as if for the enemy against which he struggled. I looked out of doors. What had happened there? Presumably it was midday, and work in the fields had stopped. Stillness and quiet had replaced the previous animation. The birds had taken themselves off to feed in the brooks. The horses stood still. Yet the power was there all the same, massed outside, indifferent, impersonal, not attending to anything in particular. Somehow it was opposed to the little hay-coloured moth. It was useless to try to do anything. One could only watch the extraordinary efforts made by those tiny legs against an oncoming doom which could, had it chosen, have submerged an entire city, not merely a city, but masses of human beings; nothing, I knew, had any chance against death. Nevertheless after a pause of exhaustion the legs fluttered again. It was superb this last protest, and so frantic that he succeeded at last in righting himself. One's sympathies, of course, were all on the side of life. Also, when there was nobody to care or to know, this gigantic effort on the part of an insignificant little moth, against a power of such magnitude, to retain what no one else valued or desired to keep, moved one strangely. Again, somehow, one saw life, a pure bead.

I lifted the pencil again, useless though I knew it to be. But even as I did so, the unmistakable tokens of death showed themselves. The body relaxed, and instantly grew stiff. The struggle was over. The insignificant little creature now knew death. As I looked at the dead moth, this minute wayside triumph of so great a force over so mean an antagonist filled me with wonder. Just as life had been strange a few minutes before, so death was now as strange. The moth having righted himself now lay most decently and uncomplainingly composed. O yes, he seemed to say, death is stronger than I am.

Photo, 2013

Orlando, 2013

Woolf Googled, 2010

Virginia Takes A Stroll
Olivia Laing

First come the deaths. The second diary entry for 1939 is about Jack Hills, her one-time brother-in-law, died Xmas Eve. *The last time I saw him was in the London Library*, she writes: rosy and stout, the same odd stammer, and she too shy to speak. His death slips her back to childhood. She thinks of her dead brother, dreams of her dead nephew, killed in Spain. The war is drawing closer; Hitler on the radio, Hitler marching into Prague. She meets Freud, who gives her a narcissus. Mark Gertler kills himself, and then a few days later, her mother-in-law *gradually ceased to breathe.*

In the midst of all this, on 18 April, a Tuesday, she starts to write a memoir. Now there are two Virginias, past and present. She sets the little one on the page, roaming about in the great wastes beneath a kitchen table. She's been worrying about ageing, worrying about the problems of biography, the way a life hardens, becomes unreal when it's put down on paper. It's not like that at all, when you're in the swim, the flush of it. She casts through the cotton wool, picking out the bright moments, the ones that glint. Which brings us to the park.

Kensington Gardens. The first thing she remembers is the woman at Gloucester Gate holding a great wobbling mass of *air balls*, coloured balloons, the same word she used in *Mrs Dalloway*. A soft quivering mass of red and purple, they come back to her whenever she sees anemones. All those walks, back and forth, have disintegrated into one. *Monotonous*, she writes. *Non-being*. This is the thing about life, the nothingness of it, and then all of a sudden the coming to.

She remembers watery things, one after another, a chain of them. First sailing a little boat on the pond with her father, both of them amazed when it sinks without warning, swallowed out of sight. Sometime later, she happens along as a keeper is dredging duckweed and so witnesses the moment – *unspeakable excitement* – when he fishes the lost boat out. But here her account founders, threatening to break down into the banal non-incident of childhood. Go-karts, chocolate, dogs tied to railings. In the slop of it, two moments emerge, rise out.

53

In the first, she remembers trying to cross a puddle. Suddenly the reality of the world falters. She can't move, can't step over. She hangs there, suspended.

In the second, she meets *an idiot boy*, into whose reaching hand she pours a bag of Russian toffees. She – the adult Virginia – types this story out, and then twice, in the space between the lines and in the margin, adds the words *with a sense of the horror*, once in a black pen and once in blue.

The encounter doesn't end there. That night in the bath the sense of horror returns to her. She huddles in the water, unable to move or speak. At the other end of the tub her sister Nessa soaps herself. *Again*, she types, *I had that hopeless sadness; that collapse I have described before; as if I were passive under some sledge hammer blow; exposed to a whole avalanche of meaning that had heaped itself up and discharged itself upon me, un-protected, with nothing to ward it off.* Discharged itself upon me, a funny turn of phrase.

Years earlier, she'd given the experience of the puddle to Rhoda in *The Waves*, who thought in her panic, her suspension in a state

of nothingness, that the only way to save herself would be to touch something hard: *Unless I can stretch and touch something hard, I shall be blown down the eternal corridors forever. What then can I touch? What brick, what stone? and so draw myself across the enormous gulf into my body safely.*

On Virginia goes, writing her way through the squares and gar-dens of her childhood. Outside, the war draws closer. On 1 November 1939, she notes in her journal another incident from Hyde Park, this time from the recent past, two days back. *On Saturday I 'saw'*, she writes, *by wh. I mean the sudden state when something moves one.* The thing she saw was a man lying on the damp grass, newspapers tucked around him. He was asleep. At his side an attaché case, and half a roll of bread. *Ought one only to write about what one 'sees' in this way*, she asks herself. It's the same question that runs right through the memoirs, which she calls *A Sketch of the Past* and leaves unfinished. These moments, these urgent moments, are they the only thing worth writing down? And what happens when they've been netted? Is their energy absorbed, are they denatured?

Perhaps not. Her next sentence: *These sights always remain.*

One last view of the park, again from the memoirs. She's thinking about how the present inflects the past, changing it day by day, mood by mood, so that anyone's history could take on almost infinite shape. Time as an oncoming tide, drowning out what's gone before. Nothing is unchangeable and so nothing is ever quite finished. How do you get that onto the page, the flickering, the quality of open-endedness? The park of her childhood threatens to recede beneath successive layers of seeings, the most recent of which came two days ago – *all the cherry trees lurid in the cold yellow light of a hail storm.*

These are not questions you can solve. These are burdens that return, interspersed by moments of lucidity, lightness like an air ball. Moving always back and forth between the formlessness, the hard and shining things. Coming closer to the water, the abyss, and then reaching at the last for something you can touch; something palpable; which might be a brick, or might – 28 March 1941 – be a stone: the kind you'd use as a paperweight, or to fasten a light thing down.

55

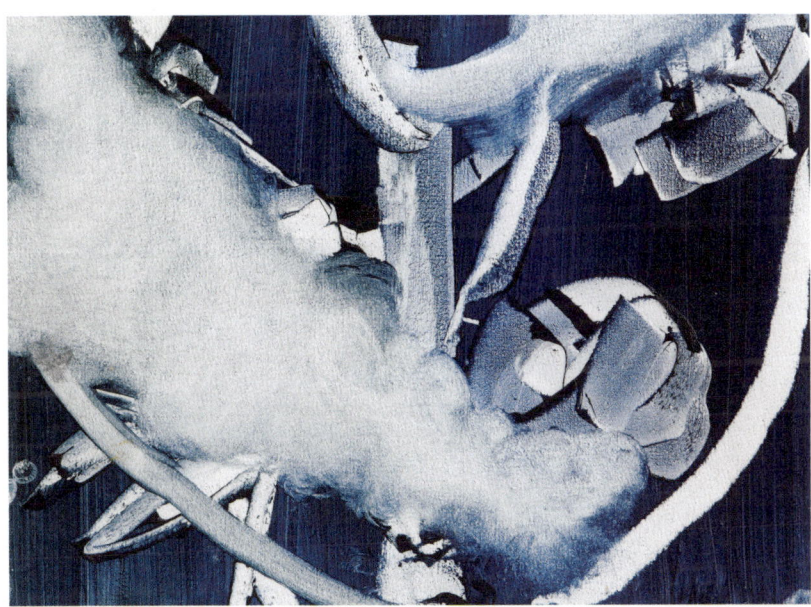

Up Here, 2003

Woolf thinking, 2010

Orlando drawing, 2013

From Flush
Virginia Woolf

Another incident a few days later showed how widely they were separated, who had been so close, how little Flush could now count on Miss Barrett for sympathy. After Mr Browning had gone one afternoon Miss Barrett decided to drive to Regent's Park with her sister. As they got out at the Park gate the door of the four-wheeler shut on Flush's paw. He 'cried piteously' and held it up to Miss Barrett for sympathy. In other days sympathy in abundance would have been lavished upon him for less. But now a detached, a mocking, a critical expression came into her eyes. She laughed at him. She thought he was shamming: '…no sooner had he touched the grass than he began to run without a thought of it', she wrote. And she commented sarcastically, 'Flush always makes the most of his misfortunes – he is of the Byronic school – *il se pose en victime*'. But here Miss Barrett, absorbed in her own emotions, misjudged him completely. If his paw had been broken, still he would have bounded. That dash was his answer to her mockery; I have done with you – that was the meaning he flashed at her as he ran. The flowers smelt bitter to him; the grass burnt his paws; the dust filled his nostrils with disillusion. But he raced – he scampered. 'Dogs must be led on chains' – there was the usual placard; there were the park-keepers with their top-hats and their truncheons to enforce it. But 'must' no longer had any meaning for him. The chain of love was broken. He would run where he liked; chase partridges; chase spaniels; splash into the middle of dahlia beds; break brilliant, blowing red and yellow roses. Let the park-keepers throw their truncheons if they chose. Let them dash his brains out. Let him fall dead, disembowelled, at Miss Barrett's feet. He cared for nothing. But naturally nothing of the kind happened. Nobody pursued him; nobody noticed him. The solitary park-keeper was talking to a nursemaid. At last he returned to Miss Barrett and she absent-mindedly slipped the chain over his neck, and led him home.

Cover of *Flush: A biography*, The Hogarth Press, 1933

Michael Landy, *Self Portrait as a Rubbish Bin*, 2012

Park Life
Amanda Coe

Two months ago, our family got a dog. There were many discussions in anticipation, as we narrowed down the ideal breed according to size, temperament and overall attractiveness – a virtual Crufts – and finally decided on an English springer spaniel. A working springer to be precise, which is a joke, since the most work this dog will ever do is to fetch a string of plastic sausages in the park. But working springers have more rounded heads than their companion breed, show springers, and during our discussions the children and I agreed an aversion to the most domed kind of spaniel head, which can resemble the bald pate of an ascetic Victorian curate. Our dog's skull is perfect: round at the top and purely canine, satiny black, with rakish splashes of white on the muzzle. We all love him, the sheer dogginess of the creature.

But, but. A dog, among all the other things it is, is a walking sack of shit. You take it on regular walks to empty it, so that its presence in your home isn't fraught with a constant sense of banal, stinking danger. The puppy book, in the austerely utopian tone of a baby-rearing manual, sets out a regime that results in a dog which 'toilets' only on command. The command the book suggests to bring this about is 'be clean!' Saying this would make me feel like the mother in *Carrie* ranting about breasts by calling them dirty pillows, so instead, my husband and I have settled on the scarcely less repressed, but certainly less embarrassing exhortation to 'be a good boy'. And, as with the baby rearing, we've opted for a more ad hoc approach than that recommended by the book, since we have lives to lead outside of breaking our dog's will until it craps on a flowerbed on command. We are not alone in this. Which is where the park comes in.

The park is, essentially, a dog toilet. Knowing this now, I quail at the memory of allowing toddlers to turn roly-polies on the piebald municipal grass, or even

61

spreading out a blanket for the odd chilly picnic, oblivious to everything beneath. Of course we bag up our dog's mess and drop it in one of the humming red enamel depositories, helpfully signed with a black dog icon, that punctuate public thoroughfares. But it may shock you to hear that not everyone does this. Some people just let their dogs defecate, freestyle, all over the green spaces Londoners see as their refuge. And our dog strains at the lead when he scents it, truffles it out, and if allowed – I'm sorry to confess – eats it. It's a puppy thing, apparently. According to the book, he'll grow out of it. I want to believe that.

Did Elizabeth Barrett (she wasn't Browning then) even take her dog, Flush, to the park? She wasn't much of a walker, suffering as she did from an enduringly mysterious illness that produced undeniable symptoms, but also relieved her of the domestic duties that were passed on to her younger sisters, freeing up EB entirely for the Life of the Mind. (I'm wondering how the sisters felt about that.) She certainly took the dog shopping (oh I see, says a Sister – Elizabeth's well enough to go *shopping*, just

not to do anything, you know, in the *house*): it was on a shopping expedition that Flush was dog-napped – one of three occasions on which he was snaffled by a gang that demanded a large ransom to return him. Barrett paid every time. She adored her spaniel, as is painfully clear from the poem 'To Flush, my Dog'. Fortunately, she wrote much better poems than this (*'Like a lady's ringlets brown/Flow thy silken ears adown'*, and so on), but perhaps none with such intensity of feeling until she fell in love with Robert Browning and had to count the ways.

The modern dog-owner may feel a glow of judgemental superiority in reading about Flush's toxic regime of sugared milk and feast-day macaroons, but the needy affection sounds just right for a spaniel (Flush was a cocker, possibly with a domed head). So did Barrett walk him? And if she did, then surely, well, Flush must have done what all dogs do? Can attendance to his bodily functions really have been delegated to an obliging footman (the Barretts were wealthy, from generations in the slave trade), armed perhaps with a discreet silver trowel?

EBB and BT, 2009

Here's the thing about having a dog. It connects you strongly to life as a creature, the needs and drives and commonality of living in a body. Perhaps this commonality seems so striking because of a dog's capacity for empathy. They feel – it appears – as we feel. If only they could speak, we say. But they are outside language; it's their charm, and their tragedy. Elizabeth Barrett lived through language more than is usual for most humans, even those who choose to be writers. She had constructed a hermetic Life of the Mind precisely because the Life of the Body was a horror for a Victorian woman; at best a chattel, at worst, murdered by incessant childbirth. But Flush, however pampered he may have been, must have forced her into a less fraught connection to the somatic. Out in Regent's Park, Barrett would have watched him adopt that comically abject squat that only means one thing, even if she never had to deal with the resulting turd. No doubt he fought other promenading dogs, or tried to hump them; he ran for the love of running. Flush was more than the love tendered to the ailing, disembodied narrator of her arduously rhymed poem. Her tribute is as much a sensuous celebration of his physicality – the 'tasselled ears', the 'dewlaps sloping' – as his devotion. So despite her own bodily self-denial, when she met Robert Browning, she was crucially prepared for more than a meeting of Minds.

The compressed, rackety third act of Elizabeth Barrett's life was a triumph: the courtship and elopement with younger, poorer Browning, the Casa Guidi years, the doted-on son (Pen!) at forty three, the popular success of *Sonnets from the Portuguese* and *Aurora Leigh*, the laudanum and séances. In the end, she fought her way to an integrated life, even if its price was estrangement from her infantilising father, avatar of Victorian Fathers. When she came to write *Aurora Leigh*, it was a dynamic rumination on the new possibility of living as both an artist and a woman: body and mind united. Flush, of course, escaped to Italy too. In a very fundamental way, he had made it all possible, beyond the pillows and the macaroons, out there in the park.

Aurora Leigh study, 2008

AURORA LEIGH

A POEM IN NINE BOOKS.

1856.

DEDICATION
TO
JOHN KENYON, Esq.

THE words "cousin" and "friend" are constantly recurring in this poem, the last pages of which have been finished under the hospitality of your roof, my own dearest cousin and friend ;—cousin and friend, in a sense of less equality and greater disinterestedness than "Romney"'s.

Ending, therefore, and preparing once more to quit England, I venture to leave in your hands this book, the most mature of my works, and the one into which my highest convictions upon Life and Art have entered ; that as, through my various efforts in Literature and steps in life, you have believed in me, borne with me, and been generous to me, far beyond the common uses of mere relationship or sympathy of mind, so you may kindly accept, in sight of the public, this poor sign of esteem, gratitude, and affection from—Your unforgetting
E. B. B.

39 DEVONSHIRE PLACE :
October 17, 1856.

AURORA LEIGH.

FIRST BOOK.

OF writing many books there is no end ;
And I who have written much in prose and
verse
For others' uses, will write now for mine,—
Will write my story for my better self,
As when you paint your portrait for a friend,
Who keeps it in a drawer and looks at it   6
Long after he has ceased to love you, just
To hold together what he was and is.

I, writing thus, am still what men call young ;
I have not so far left the coasts of life   10
To travel inland, that I cannot hear
That murmur of the outer Infinite
Which unweaned babies smile at in their sleep
When wondered at for smiling ; not so far,
But still I catch my mother at her post   15
Beside the nursery door, with finger up,
"Hush, hush—here's too much noise !"
while her sweet eyes
Leap forward, taking part against her word
In the child's riot.   Still I sit and feel
My father's slow hand, when she had left us
both,   20
Stroke out my childish curls across his knee,
And hear Assunta's daily jest (she knew
He liked it better than a better jest)
Inquire how many golden scudi went   24
To make such ringlets.   O my father's hand,
Stroke heavily, heavily the poor hair down,
Draw, press the child's head closer to thy
knee !
I'm still too young, too young, to sit alone.

I write.   My mother was a Florentine,   29
Whose rare blue eyes were shut from seeing me
When scarcely I was four years old, my life
A poor spark snatched up from a failing lamp
Which went out therefore.   She was weak
and frail ;
She could not bear the joy of giving life,
The mother's rapture slew her.   If her kiss
Had left a longer weight upon my lips   36
It might have steadied the uneasy breath,
And reconciled and fraternised my soul
With the new order.   As it was, indeed,
I felt a mother-want about the world,   40
And still went seeking, like a bleating lamb
Left out at night in shutting up the fold,—

352

The Vision of Aurora Leigh, 2007

Birds, 2004

Bridge Fishers
Iain Sinclair

Our expeditions usually begin at first light. This time, Stephen explained, we would do better to hold off until the worst of the rush hour had burnt itself out. I sat on the church porch and waited, admiring a procession of those bright-red sculptural interventions held long enough at the traffic lights to catch the appreciative eye, the new Stagecoach buses with the NOT IN SERVICE destination windows. Pristine, denuded of human mess, the buses were like bricks of tin turned on their side, picture windows gleaming. Stalled under the railway bridge and shuddering slightly, like overbred racehorses, this convoy of scarlet cardinals basked in autumn sunlight in their aura of expensive entitlement.

It was good to be alive and out in the streets again. Launched on another adventure. Our part of the city had, over recent years, stopped being a discarded library book filled with obscure facts and teasing memorials to dead writers, and was currently rebranded as a perpetually overpainted, self-cannibalising graffiti gallery. Authentic vagrants and rough sleepers, the ones who had not been rationalised to somewhere more attractive, like Glasgow, Stoke-on-Trent, Lowestoft, now existed as quotations. I noticed that a poster inviting us to 'make poverty history' had been improved with an aerosol representation of a life-sized Orwellian tramp hunched up on the pavement. A passing spray merchant had then signed the whole complex piece, with its layers of competitive signage, with a large blue autograph. The poster covered the space of a hidden door.

'I love that blue, the way it's disappearing.'

Stephen's art – and I regard him as a major resource, a master of the territory – is about love. Discriminations of love. Love as anger. Love as *notice*, staying alert to flaws, follies, civic impositions. He catalogues the spectacularly mundane: junked betting slips, cans of energy drinks, albums of wedding photographs. But, as a lesson to me, my jaundiced vision, he is always positive. His work is as much an excuse to be out there, on the move, tramping, cycling, pumping up his kayak, hopping a random train, as a requirement to make prints, put out books, curate exhibitions. Take away his camera and he'd draw with a felt-tip pen on his eyeballs.

'Years of Bethnal Green sunlight went into making that colour. The blue has faded so beautifully.'

Stephen is one of the few people to appreciate the old railway bridges *as bridges*. As unofficial gates or portals to the next zone of London. He logs them, he registers them. He goes out early to do it. But today his new project requires a later start. He'll be standing in the middle of the road poking a long pole into the hidden crannies under a succession of local railway bridges. There are many bridges, many tunnels. Feathers, fallen nests. Ooze and reek.

We walk west.

My guide is dressed like an urban fisherman: soft blue hat with no flies in the band, blue protective jacket, loose trousers, heavy boots. He is carrying a bulging bag and a silver pole. He

calls a halt where Collingwood Street emerges from Three Colts Lane. (I've never been sure if that name derived from runaway gypsy horses, or if you needed three Colt pistols in your belt to make safe passage.)

'Look at that,' Stephen says.

The lovely arched roof of the tunnel under the railway is scratched with claw marks, long yellow-orange striations revealing the original glow of the bricks beneath generations of thick grey sludge-varnish.

'Overloaded vans heading south to the scrap yards,' Stephen reveals.

The white goods heaped on numerous Transits had gouged at the curve of the low ceiling. The lane going north was untouched. Stephen was a connoisseur of blight, but this bridge didn't answer. It was not a promising spot to begin our fishing. He knew the ways of the river-roads and the silver streams of the railways as a true native. A hunter-gatherer of images. On our walk from Cambridge Heath Road, he pointed out the remediated warehouse where he had kept a studio for many years; the site from which he had launched his dawn raids on disputed terrain.

Stephen Gill, from *Pigeons Book*, 2012

The former inhabitants had been priced out, then expelled: all those fugitive activities, printers, photographers, invisibles. Even the junkies shooting up in the metal box of the lift.

'I was on the spot. I could watch the trains from my window. I could cycle off up the Lea Valley. I could work all night in the darkroom, sleep in the studio. Go for a wash to York Hall.'

And now? Enclosed. Scaffolded. Another investment opportunity. Make your purchase, sight unseen, in Kuala Lumpur.

The silver fishing pole is extended. Stephen is happy with this new pitch, the pool of shimmering ghost-light under the second bridge.

'Listen,' he says. 'Feel it. The ripple and shudder of the Stansted Express.'

Planks tremble. Girders sigh. Now his pole looks like the prosthetic arm of a manic soundman trying to capture the hiss of expanding metal joists. He purchased it, so he told me, in a useful hardware shop on Hackney Road. The telescopic pole is intended for use by window-cleaners. Stephen has adapted it for his camera. We don't need to see the prey, we can smell them: like burnt marzipan blended with diesel soup. Like lung-peeling ammonia. Like marsh gas trapped in the bones of a plague pit. Like unsponsored, unregistered, post-historic London. Stephen has the clothes, the camera, the whippy rod. He's forgotten the surgical facemask. The reluctant subjects of his investigation are the tribes of feral pigeons that have infested these arches since the coming of the railways. They have seen the days of trading in exotic animals, lion cubs, parrots, monkeys, come and go.

The peculiar and unquantifiable magic of the area derives from the Victorian invasion by canals and railways: secret caves for dealers, hucksters, illegitimates. Stephen is celebrating the private life of the much maligned pigeon colonies. He achieves the only sequence I know that carries its own paper-eating smell: grey and spectral coops within the dignified ironwork of the railway's epic engineering. Birds are like dead souls nesting on stalagmites, on conical reefs and mounds of their own droppings. Aeons of acid excrement eating into metal. We have never witnessed these creatures in such enclosed settings:

so defenceless, taken by stealth. They are ruffled, agitated by the shock of the harsh flash. The avian portraits, over which Stephen has limited control, are pure revelation. They chart previously unrecorded London life; one of those tiny pockets left outside the intrusion of surveillance systems.

Pilgrims, mostly Asian, passing through the tunnel as through a border crossing between worlds, notice the image-fisher, but choose to leave him alone, without comment. The long pole wavers. Stephen stands, he raids. Traffic swerves. He counts aloud, his camera is primed: 'One-two-three...' After twelve seconds, the flash detonates. Stephen is shooting blind. He won't know what he's got until he makes the print. All too often, the birds explode in an aggrieved spatter of wings, like the sound of a reverberating chamber of ironic applause. They circle, swoop, settle, regroup on the steep roof of new flats erected in place of the Vallance Road terrace where the Kray family once made their headquarters. Such souls as managed to transmigrate from that dark period have another existence in pigeon purgatory.

A young bird, fallen from the nest, still pink of belly, thrashes on a ledge, unable, so it seems, to take flight, but unwilling to fall to the ground; trapped in restless Sisyphean torment. A metaphor for some of the horrors of place. With nothing to be done.

The strangest aspect of Stephen's pigeon séance is that nobody challenges us, two men poking a silver rod up under a railway bridge. A rod with a camera attachment. And a brutal flash (the kind that conspiracy theorists claim blinded Princess Di's driver in the underpass). In surveillance city, where public image-making is seen as suspect, if not criminal – 'Don't you know there's a war on?' – fishing for pigeon portraits passes without comment. Until a local matron, dog on a string, approaches.

'You're doing it wrong, gentlemen. You'll never get rid of them that way. I've lived here thirty years and I've tried everything. But they still land on my head every time I set foot on the street. They think they fucking own the place.'

73

From
Frankenstein
Mary Shelley

'How can I move thee? Will no intreaties cause thee to turn a favourable eye upon thy creature, who implores thy goodness and compassion? Believe me, Frankenstein: I was benevolent; my soul glowed with love and humanity; but am I not alone, miserably alone? You, my creator, abhor me; what hope can I gather from your fellow-creatures, who owe me nothing? They spurn and hate me. The desert mountains and dreary glaciers are my refuge. I have wandered here many days; the caves of ice, which I only do not fear, are a dwelling to me, and the only one which man does not grudge. These bleak skies I hail, for they are kinder to me than your fellow beings. If the multitude of mankind knew of my existence, they would do as you do, and arm themselves for my destruction. Shall I not then hate them who abhor me? I will keep no terms with my enemies. I am miserable, and they shall share my wretchedness. Yet it is in your power to recompense me, and deliver them from an evil which it only remains for you to make so great, that not only you and your family, but thousands of others, shall be swallowed up in the whirlwinds of its rage. Let your compassion be moved, and do not disdain me. Listen to my tale: when you have heard that, abandon or commiserate me, as you shall judge that I deserve. But hear me. The guilty are allowed, by human laws, bloody as they are, to speak in their own defence before they are condemned. Listen to me, Frankenstein. You accuse me of murder, and yet you would, with a satisfied conscience, destroy your own creature. Oh, praise the eternal justice of man! Yet I ask you not to spare me: listen to me, and then, if you can, and if you will, destroy the work of your hands.'

Gesture, 2007

Shelley, 2013

The Poet, 2008

Frances Burney

From
The Apprentice Years: 35
Frances Burney

From Letter to Samuel Crisp, April 1776

Mr Burney, Heey and I took a walk in the Park on Sunday morning, where, among others, we saw the young and handsome Duchess of Devonshire, walking in such an undressed and slatternly manner as, in former Times, Mrs Rishton might have done in Chesington Garden. Two of her Curls came quite Unpinned, and fell lank on One of her shoulders; one shoe was down at Heel, the Trimming of her Jacket and coat was in some places unsewn; her Cap was awry and her cloak, which was rusty and powdered, was flung half on and half off. Had she not had a servant in superb Livery behind her, she would certainly have been affronted.[1] Every creature turned back to stare at her. Indeed I think her very handsome, and she has a look of innocence and artlessness that made me quite sorry she should be so foolishly negligent of her Person. She had hold of the Duke's arm, who is the very reverse of herself, for he is ugly, tidy, and grave. He looks like a very mean shop keeper's Journey man.

Omai, who was in the Park, called here this morning, and says that he went to her Grace, and asked her why she let her Hair go in that manner? Ha, Ha, Ha, – don't you Laugh at her having a Lesson of Attention from an Otaheitan?

. As a loose woman, or a prostitute. Georgina Spencer had at seventeen married the fifth Duke of Devonshire. Now tow years later, she was a famous beauty whose charm and ebullience made her a leading figure in London society. For a woman of her social stature she was unusually informal and unaffected, which, coupled with her youth, probably accounts for her unkempt dress on this occasion.

Cover of *Evelina* by Fanny Burney

Fanny Burney thinks her Hat into a Rose, 2013

John Stezaker, *Mask XIII*, 2006

George Eliot

Inner and Outer
Emily Rhodes

About five o'clock I could not help pausing and exclaiming at the exquisite beauty of the light on Regent's Park, exalting it into something that the young Turner would have wanted to paint.

George Eliot wrote this in a letter to her friend Barbara Bodichon, after a visit to London Zoo in September 1868. Her reference to Turner would have resonated with Madame Bodichon, who was an artist as well as a campaigner for women's education. It conjures light flooding the canvas, gesturing towards the sublime – an intense beauty that overwhelms the polite setting of Regent's Park.

For Regent's Park is nothing if not polite. It is where man coerces nature into art, sculpts wildness into a landscape fit for society's enjoyment. Nature's uneven gluts and scarcities are transformed into neat, formal gardens; the River Tyburn is turned into a boating lake; the entire park is bound by the rings of its Inner and Outer Circles.

On this September afternoon, Eliot saw nature's beauty break free from the double bonds of Regent's Park. The 'exquisite light' gave nature sufficient force to transcend man's attempt to contain it, yielding a Turneresque encounter with the sublime.

Another of Eliot's transcendent lights comes at the start of her Prelude to *Middlemarch*. Saint Theresa was a woman whose 'flame ... soared after some illimitable satisfaction, some object which would never justify weariness, which would reconcile self-despair with the rapturous consciousness of life beyond self'. 'What,' asks Eliot, 'were the many-volumed romances of chivalry and the social conquests of a brilliant girl to her?' Saint Theresa's 'passionate, ideal nature demanded an epic life', free from society's 'coiffured' arrangement. Like the sun on Regent's Park and the light of Turner's paintings, her flame burned through its bonds, enabling her to find 'her epos in the reform of a religious order'.

Virginia Woolf described Eliot as a woman who, like Saint

Theresa, stretched beyond her allotted place:

> The burdens and complexities of womanhood were not enough; she must reach beyond the sanctuary and pluck for herself the strange bright fruits of art and knowledge.

Eliot 'found her epos' in her wonderful novels – the 'strange bright fruits' of her literary career. She also reached 'beyond the sanctuary' in her scandalous openness about her relationship with Lewes, a married man. This illicit relationship was enjoyed beyond society's bounds, both morally and geographically. Rather than settling in a fashionable area of London, Eliot and Lewes lived in the bohemian suburb of St John's Wood, just north of Regent's Park. If the park, on the city's edge, was where nature was made palatable for society, in St John's Wood it could be a little more wild.

What, though, of those women whose flames were mere 'dim lights', not fierce enough to blaze through society's bonds? What of those who didn't make their homes on society's edge, but were trapped in its heart? What of a latter-day Saint Theresa caught in polite Middlemarch?

Dorothea Brooke shares Saint Theresa's 'passionate, ideal nature', but her flame doesn't soar. Stifled by society, she is:

> Foundress of nothing, whose loving heart-beats and sobs after an unattained goodness tremble off and are dispersed among hindrances, instead of centring in some long-recognizable deed.

At least this is how she is portrayed in the Prelude. By the time we reach the end of *Middlemarch*, Eliot's view has shifted. Rather than the bleak forecast of Dorothea's goodness uselessly 'dispersed among hindrances', Eliot says her effect on those around her was 'incalculably diffusive'. 'The growing good of the world', she continues, 'is partly dependent on unhistoric acts'. Perhaps, then, Saint Theresa's soaring flame is no more important than the diffuse light of Dorothea's 'unhistoric acts'.

The dim flicker of a candle flame has its own benefits, as Eliot tells us elsewhere in *Middlemarch*:

> Your pier-glass or extensive surface of polished steel made to

Gibbous Moon, 2007

be rubbed by a housemaid, will be minutely and multitudinously scratched in all directions; but place now against it a lighted candle as a centre of illumination, and lo! the scratches will seem to arrange themselves in a fine series of concentric circles round that little sun.

The lighted candle is a 'sun', but only a 'little' one. It doesn't blaze through Regent's Park, overwhelming the viewer with the sublime, but is contained within a neat arrangement of concentric circles.

In Regent's Park, nature's wild power is dimmed by the double bonds of Inner and Outer Circles, and yet beauty still glows within those bounds. With each unrehearsed unfurling of a petal or turn of a leaf, the park glitters with life, albeit contained in tidy flower beds. The park is never quite enthralled by man's design. No matter how many times he tries to circumscribe it, beauty and goodness remain in each tiny 'unhistoric act'. Its effect is 'incalculably diffusive', rippling ever outwards like the concentric circles from Dorothea's candle flame.

Every character, says Eliot, has 'an equivalent centre of self, whence the lights and shadows must always fall with a certain difference'. She moves between her characters – her many 'little suns' – demonstrating how the scratches arrange themselves around one, and then another. She invites her readers to identify with Dorothea, but also sympathise with Casaubon; even such minor characters as Bulstrode are given convincing minds of their own. Eliot gives us the intricate freedom of empathy, enabling us to step outside the concentric circles of one candle flame and into a different, but equivalent, pool of light. Empathy is, for Eliot, the function of art: to 'amplify experience and extend our contact with our fellow-men beyond the bounds of our personal lot'. Her novels are universes of many little suns, fictions in which no candle flame eclipses another.

So much for Dorothea and the other flickering candles who inhabit *Middlemarch*, but what of Saint Theresa's bright flame? She appears only in the novel's Prelude and Finale, and is markedly absent from the main body of *Middlemarch*. She cannot be held within Eliot's fiction, and she would certainly not be contained in this domestic scene of pier-glass and housemaid-polished surfaces. Saint Theresa's flame would burn the house down.

George Eliot created remarkable fictions populated with the flickering lights of many equivalent centres of self, but she did not hope to contain real suns – incandescent and certainly not 'little'. Saint Theresa is outside the bounds of *Middlemarch*, just as Eliot lived 'beyond the sanctuary' of society. They are soaring flames, akin to the light on Regent's Park on that September afternoon, 'something that the young Turner would have wanted to paint'. Inner and Outer Circles disappear in the rare blaze of the sublime.

Moth, 2010

Laura Braun, *Oak Tree*

Eliot, 2011

entered into everybody's food; it was fermenting still as a distinguishable vigorous enthusiasm in certain long-haired German artists at Rome, and the youth of other nations who worked or idled near them were sometimes caught in the spreading movement.

One fine morning a young man whose hair was not immoderately long, but abundant and curly, and who was otherwise English in his equipment, had just turned his back on the Belvedere Torso in the Vatican and was looking out on the magnificent view of the mountains from the adjoining round vestibule. He was sufficiently absorbed not to notice the approach of a dark-eyed, animated German who came up to him and placing a hand on his shoulder, said with a strong accent, " Come here, quick ! else she will have changed her pose."

Quickness was ready at the call, and the two figures passed lightly along by the Meleager towards the hall where the reclining Ariadne, then called the Cleopatra, lies in the marble voluptuousness of her beauty, the drapery folding around her with a petal-like ease and tenderness. They were just in time to see another figure standing against a pedestal near the reclining marble: a breathing blooming girl, whose form, not shamed by the Ariadne, was clad in Quakerish grey drapery;

Middlemarch, George Eliot, 1871-2

her long cloak, fastened at the neck, was thrown
backward from her arms, and one beautiful un-
gloved hand pillowed her cheek, pushing somewhat backward the white beaver bonnet which
made a sort of halo to her face around the simply
braided dark-brown hair.   She was not looking at
the sculpture, probably not thinking of it: her
large eyes were fixed dreamily on a streak of sunlight which fell across the floor.   But she became
conscious of the two strangers who suddenly
paused as if to contemplate the Cleopatra, and,
without looking at them, immediately turned away
to join a maid-servant and courier who were loiter-
ing along the hall at a little distance off.

"What do you think of that for a fine bit of
antithesis?" said the German, searching in his
friend's face for responding admiration, but going
on volubly without waiting for any other answer.
"There lies antique beauty, not corpse-like even
in death, but arrested in the complete contentment
of its sensuous perfection: and here stands beauty
in its breathing life, with the consciousness of
Christian centuries in its bosom.   But she should
be dressed as a nun; I think she looks almost
what you call a Quaker; I would dress her as a
nun in my picture.   However, she is married; I
saw her wedding-ring on that wonderful left hand,

VOL. I.   Z

Triton, 2006

Interlude

The Speakers
Craig Taylor

'In the 1930s,' Gordon said, 'a shooting range for machine guns was built in Hyde Park, not far from Speakers' Corner. It was used by the gentry who lived in the houses near South Audley Street, until one afternoon a Browning swivelled too far on its pivot and somewhere in the distance a horse's foreleg burst. In the early 1940s, residents of Edgware Road often gathered of a Sunday morning in the autumn in Hyde Park when the leaves themselves were starting to resemble fire. Near North Carriage Drive they set alight effigies of Adolf Hitler, which had been hung from the lower branches of the plane trees. Some were stuffed with concoctions of soaked rags and even offal, so they hissed and popped as the flame crept over the fabric. Preparation commenced weeks beforehand, often in the small hours of the blackout. Neighbour competed against neighbour to craft the most authentic doppelgänger, and later picnics sprung up across the park as the Hitlers smouldered, and sing-songs drifted on the air along with the threads of smoke.

'In the late 1960s, Mick Jagger was said to have sold his soul in an elaborate ceremony at the crossroads near the Speke Monument. He buried a live chicken in the soil, under cover of night, while allegedly high on something, and surrounded by a coterie of curious and beautiful hangers-on, all women, all of whom were sworn to secrecy. One disclosed the secret years later. By that time she was living alone in Harrow, still beautiful, but sinewy – you know that look – and disillusioned by years with the Stones and all that came after, especially the nights of the 1980s in dank Camden pubs with men who assured her they had just joined Black Sabbath, they would be on the next tour, they'd be playing bass guitar. But nothing could match the evenings with the Stones. She still remembered Hyde Park that night, Jagger's hands covered in blood, stretched up into the

93

night, begging the gods of London to grant him immortality.'

'To grant him what?' I asked. I couldn't always hear Gordon's voice over the sounds of the traffic as we walked.

'Immortality, and,' Gordon said to me, 'those three were just off the top of my head. If they were still curious after hearing those, then I told them other lies, often just to see their reaction. Ninety per cent of what I told customers on those guided London walks,' he said, 'was true. I was a good guide, but some days it was as if they needed another fact to complete the experience. On other days I was just bored of repeating the walk, the same explanations, the same pauses, and it became difficult to enjoy the punchlines. I used to think a tourist might say to me: "Gordon, I've actually read most of the Rolling Stones biographies and no one ever mentions a ceremony in Hyde Park. No one mentions chicken blood." I would have loved a challenge, but for the most part they smiled politely at me. I could have scuffed a bit of soil and called it the shallow grave of the Queen Mother and they would have nodded, checked their battery level and photographed the dirt. Occasionally someone would say: "Are you an actor when you're not leading these walks?" and I'd say yes. "Shakespearean?" they'd ask. And I'd say: mostly children's theatre, but of the sort that deals with heavier themes. After that I'd become even more trustworthy in their eyes,' Gordon said. He pointed west along the pavement of Oxford Street. 'We should cross over to the other side.'

So we did, and continued our walk towards Marble Arch.

'Occasionally,' Gordon told me as he began walking on the pavement again, 'one of the tourists on my London walks would say to me: "Could you take us all the way through Hyde Park?" But I liked to keep the tours short. I liked to look at Hyde Park from a distance. You couldn't take these tourists into its depths. If I walked a group all the way through Hyde Park they would cling together. They would have no chance to leave me. Not with grace. They couldn't just fade into a street or a pub.'

'How did they pay you?' I asked him.

'They paid per walk.'

'At the beginning?'

'You get the money off them at the start,' Gordon said. 'So you can let them go. Some are only interested in the beginning.'

We walked through the underground tunnels at Marble Arch. An enormous bronze statue of a horse's head had been installed at the Marble Arch roundabout. It looked like the horse was drinking; its lips touched the plinth, but barely, those rubbery horse lips made from bronze. The name of the piece is *Still Water* and I nearly took a photo on my phone when we approached. I stopped because Gordon was there and instead stepped up onto the podium and laid my hand on the horse's cheek and even pressed my palm into its cold bronze nostril. I've looked at it online since, but there's nothing constant in the photos that come up in an image search, as the horse head in some is mint green and others dirty grey. The streaks drift across from photo to photo, and it's not just because of the time of day. In one photo the artist stands on a cherrypicker washing away white swathes of pigeon shit. In another, the horse head is nearly black, set in shadow by the London sunset behind, as the sun descends beyond the park, and now that I've downloaded that photo and stuck it with my own, in a miscellaneous folder with personal photos, I tend to look back fondly on that sunset.

We crossed the street and entered the park and soon heard the women on rented bikes call out 'Sorry' as they teetered by. Morning sunlight made the canvas of the rental chairs glow; it wasn't yet noon. The speakers of Speakers' Corner had assembled. 'A wind,' Gordon said as we moved through the crowd, 'shakes the plane leaves. The hiss obscures the preacher's voice.' Which was true, or nearly. A tour group surrounded one preacher, although surely they couldn't hear what he was saying. A few of the preachers had tucked sound systems under their stepladders. We didn't need to listen to the preachers today. The wind acted as a natural shush, and sounded even more forceful here at Speakers' Corner. When the wind dropped, Arabic pop leaked in from one of the sound systems, and was then erased by another gust.

'All the First World countries drink . . .' one of the tourists

95

yelled out to the Muslim speaker atop the stepladder as we passed.

'*Haram*,' the speaker replied.

'All the first world countries...'

'Alcohol is *haram*. It brings on misery.'

Joggers wearing rucksacks pushed through the crowd. Pigeons took flight and were rebuffed by the wind. Years ago I'd come to Speakers' Corner with my other flatmate Jerome, just the two of us, with Gordon nowhere in sight. On that visit we stayed and watched each of the preachers in turn. We moved from one to the next. 'This is where I come,' Jerome had told me, 'when I want to feel proud of how rich and godless my life is because gathered here on Sundays are the worst of the worst.' Even back in 2010, the preachers came with stepladders adorned with B&Q price stickers. Some lay cloth over plastic milk crates and neatly folded the jutting edges. On the Sunday Jerome took me to Speakers' Corner I saw an American evangelist dressed in a cape hoist himself onto a wooden box where he told us the strength of the American God would ensure his safety for the length of the speech. A few minutes in he turned his head while pointing at

one of the Muslims. He looked like the American preacher who had picketed the funerals of dead soldiers a few years ago, but our man was younger, more theatrical, and he shook his cape around to reveal the word Jesus written in sequins. It was then that I said to Jerome, 'I think I've had enough.' He said 'Let's stay.'

So we did. One of the Muslim guys had no audience. He made a hissing sound each time he said Israel. Jerome stood in front for a few minutes. When we finally walked on, the speaker yelled out Israel again, and continued to speak to the backs of others, until he was drowned out. When we reached the rental chairs, which were full of sunbathers that time of year, I said to Jerome, 'Can we see the park now?'

He nodded. He was too warmly dressed for summer, one too many layers. He was pale and blinking in the light. The preaching was winding down. Some of the speakers left without ceremony. Two or three faded away as if by agreement with each other. Another two embarked on loud final statements, aided by their supporters. They spoke from high on their stepladders, arms raised, until one finished,

Park

and then the other finished. That same American was there on that day in 2010. He had to descend from his ladder, gather his material, bend over and gather pamphlets, hide them in a coat pocket, bend over again, gather his cape into a greying plastic bag. He started to walk back to Marble Arch. His one remaining believer folded and carried the ladder and ran to catch up. 'The ladder carriers,' Jerome said.

The November wind kept shushing us as we walked. Gordon had used packing tape on the cylinder containing Jerome's ashes. 'On one of my walking tours,' Gordon tried to say above the rush of the plane leaves, but he was drowned out.

We walked away from Speakers' Corner, into the park. He walked towards the edge of the pavement, away from the preachers and onto the grass.

'On one of the walking tours,' Gordon said, 'I remember someone asking, "Does anyone get trampled by the horses on Rotten Row?"'

'It's probably happened.'

'It probably has, you know.'

Further into the park Gordon chose a spot underneath a plane tree. When he set down the

rucksack and opened the zipper I caught a glimpse of a metal utensil tucked inside. I offered to take it.

'I've got it,' he said.

'Isn't that thing meant for poaching eggs?' I asked.

'That's not its only use.'

He held the taped-up cylinder and began cutting the seal with his Swiss Army knife. He left the egg-poacher poking out of the rucksack.

He unwrapped the last of the tape.

After it was done, Gordon said, 'You know, the groundskeepers who work in the park say they'll often find a pile here or there, just a pile of ashes, as if people just tip the container and walk away. Informally, they don't mind people leaving the stuff here but you've got to spread it. You have to use a utensil. Some mornings you can see mounds, they say. Seriously. The rain doesn't get rid of them. The mounds can burn away a patch of earth. The phosphates can do terrible things to the earth.'

'Is that true?'

'I'm sure it is.'

I went to pick up the implement he had used for the spreading, but Gordon took it first.

'I can help,' I said.

'It's all right,' he replied.

He gathered up the cylinder. He fixed his cuffs. He wrapped the implement in a tea towel and stowed it in his rucksack, put the rucksack on and dealt with his cuffs again. We stood there. As per old wishes, I remained silent, not a word, not a thought, not a prayer, nothing but air through the plane trees.

'It's calcium too,' said Gordon. 'You can imagine. It would damage the soil if it's not spread. Though I don't know the science.'

Crimson Leaf, 2011

Can't Give you Anything but Love, 2013

From Love
Angela Carter

One day Annabel saw the sun and moon in the sky at the same time. The sight filled her with a terror which entirely consumed her and did not leave her until the night closed in catastrophe for she had no instinct for self-preservation if she was confronted by ambiguities.

It had happened as she walked home through the park. In the system of correspondences by which she interpreted the world around her, this park had a special significance and she walked along its overgrown paths with nervous pleasure, especially in certain yellow, tarnished lights of the branches with cold fire. An eighteenth-century landscape gardener planned the park to surround a mansion which had been pulled down long ago and now the once harmonious artificial wilderness, randomly dishevelled by time, speaks it green tangles across the high shoulder of a hill only a stone's throw from a busy road that ran through the city dockland. All that remained of the former mansion were a few architectural accessories now the property of the city museum. There was a stable built on the lines of a miniature Parthenon, housing for Houyhnhnms rather than natural horses; the pillared portico, especially effective under the light of a full moon, never to be entered again by any horse, functioned only as a pure piece of design, a focal point in the green composition on the south side of the hill where Annabel rarely ventured for serenity bored her and the Mediterranean aspect of the park held no excitements for her. She preferred the Gothic north, where an ivy-covered tower with leaded ogive windows skulked among the trees. Both these pretty whimsies were kept securely locked for fear of the despoliation of vandals but their presence still performed its original role, transforming the park into a premeditated theatre where the romantic imagination could act out any performance it chose amongst settings of classic harmony or crabbed quaintness. And the magic strangeness of the park was enhanced by its curious silence. Footfalls fell softly on the long grass and few birds sang there, but the presence all around of the sprawling, turbulent city, however muffled its noises, lent such haunted, breathless quiet an unnatural quality.

The park maintained only a single, still impressive entrance, a massive pair of wrought-iron gates decorated with cherubs, marks of beasts, stylised reptiles and spearheads from which the gilding flakes, but these gates were never either open or closed. They hung always a little ajar and dropped from their hinges with age; they served a function no longer for all the railings round the park were gone long ago and access everywhere was free and easy. The park was on such high ground it seemed to hang in the air above a vast, misty model of a city and those who walked through it always felt excessively exposed to the weather. At times, all seemed nothing but a playground for the winds and, at others, an immense rain for all the rain the heavens could pour forth.

Annabel went through the park in a season of high winds and lurid weather, early one winter's evening, and happened to look up at the sky. On her right, she saw the sun shining down on the district of terraces and crescents where she lived while, on her left, above the spires and skyscrapers of the city itself, the rising moon hung motionless in a rift of absolute night. Though one was setting while the other rose, both sun and moon gave forth an equal brilliance so the heavens contained two contrary states at once. Annabel gazed upwards, appalled to see such a dreadful rebellion of the familiar. There was nothing in her mythology to help her resolve this conflict and, all at once, she felt herself the helpless pivot of the entire universe as if sun, moon, stars and all the hosts of the sky span around upon herself, their volitionless axle.

Fountain girls, 2006

X What would 'Nora
me have done

Wise Children: One.
~~Overture a beginners~~

Why is London like Budapest? Because it is two cities divided by a river.

*

You used to be able to make a crude distinction - the rich lived on the North bank, amongst pleasant verdure with abundant public transport, & the poor lived on the South bank in circumstances of arid deprivation, condemned, to wait for hours at windswept bus stops whilst partially feral cats marauded dustbins & resources of marital violence made the night hideous. ~~as they echoed through the~~ Things are more complicated, now; ~~the Thames~~ "posts" the division a little less clearcut - there's been a diaspora of the affluent, they've scattered all ~~over~~ over the city, that's what happens when property values go through the roof, ~~in the~~ And what does the robin do then, poor thing.

Bugger the robin. X If my mum hadn't had the sense to buy this house, knock down price, during the Blitz, ~~if she hadn't~~ we'd be ~~out~~ on the streets now, Nora & me, pushing our worldlies up & down on supermarket trollies, reduced to sucking on the bottle for comfort like babes unweaned & no doubt intermittently bursting into uninvited song XX when finally allowed admittance to the night shelter & so chucked out to freeze on the midnight street again. That's the apolyphic scenario, of course; XX we always knew we had the house to fall back on, see, so we never bothered to put a bit away. Easy come, easy go, that was the motto of the Chance girls. The "Lucky Chances."   X when our girls came in

XX out of pure joy & relief   *

X if they wanted release from the transpontine limbo

Can't Give you Anything but Love, detail, 2013

Park 5, 2004

Sarah Pickstone
Marina Warner

A famous painting of an artist at work shows the German Romantic Caspar David Friedrich standing with his back to a window that is shuttered against the view, the light coming in from the top half where only the sky is visible. The portrait is by a friend of the painter's, Georg Kersting, and he was keeping faith with Friedrich's practice of cultivating his mind's eye and drawing on memory and imagination to create his scenes of nature. Friedrich took this aesthetic principle very far, far farther than Sarah Pickstone, for she makes preparatory sketches from the scene and later develops them in the studio; but solitude and an intense process of crystallising mental images are central to her working methods.

Sarah Pickstone's London studio is an enclosed, top lit, walled enclave, but its walls vanish into the scenes she has painted on surfaces that fill them almost completely. Entering her workspace, I found that I passed from one zone into another – a different place where light and air exist as colour and clarity, as *illumination* in the strong, wide-ranging sense of the term.

'The Writers Series', the project Sarah began in 2009, is inspired by Regent's Park and by the writers – the women writers – who have walked there and thought there. The way Sarah evokes the park as a spring of female creativity and imagination intensified the sense I already had of stepping across a threshold into somewhere else – not because the studio was safe or warm, or anything simply creaturely and comfortable, but because her paintings transform a concrete box into a place of delicate yet intense illumination – a diaphane, made up of the subtle texture of memories, that material immateriality of flames and rainbows and beams of light. (As an aside, it is not uninteresting that *Les Illuminations*, Rimbaud's extraordinary sequence of prose poems, was written in London when he was living in Camden Town with Verlaine, not far from Regent's Park, and he intended the French title to be read in English.)

Sarah Pickstone speaks of the park as a realm on its own terms, neither a garden nor the countryside, neither a landscape nor a wilderness, but something in-between. It is bounded, urban, and it springs surprises: a 'multiplicity' (her word) of possibilities exists within its boundaries.

There are hidden enclaves – like the Secret Garden where the artist sometimes goes to draw. The statue of Hylas at the centre of this inner sanctum appears in several of her paintings, an emblem of mythic presence in the park, a carrier of enigmatic story. In the classical tale, Hylas, an ambiguous boy-girl, was captured by nymphs who fell in

Cover of Rimbaud's *Oeuvres Poétiques*, 1964

love with him, and taken down into the depths. He also appears, in a very different style, in J. W. Waterhouse's eroticised painting, which hangs in the Manchester Art Gallery (Pickstone's home town). Sarah Pickstone's Hylas draws lightly on these layers of association, and she paints the statue enigmatically mirrored – drowned – in the fountain.

The artist has turned her observations of the park from urban pastoral into poetic summonses of writers and of the mood and feel of their works. She has portrayed in this way Elizabeth Barrett Browning, Virginia Woolf, Katherine Mansfield, Sylvia Plath, Stevie Smith, and evoked others through emblems – artists' palettes, for example. In a painting paying tribute to Angela Carter's *Wise Children*, she includes a proscenium arch to salute the theatrical exuberance and love of theatre in that pyro-technical novel about London and Londoners. The park was the haunt of all these writers and the setting of scenes in their works to different degrees and in varying ways; they return as characters in the paintings not to induce a spectral frisson, but as ravishing figments, the visual equivalent of

their disembodied voice on the page.

In the past Sarah has used 'Figment' as the title of a painting, and she likes to keep her paint facture flat, often using aluminium sheets for 'canvas', the metal's satiny smoothness allowing her brushstrokes and their burden of paint to appear insubstantial, wraith-like, with affinities to transparent petals and sepals and the wings of moths. The delicacy of touch sets questions stirring in us, about yearning, transience, and fragility – and about her subjects and herself as women. Are there elements here of seeing-as-a-woman, of touching-as-a-woman?

Virginia Woolf, a voice of crucial inspiration to Sarah, also caught impressions on the wing, the subtle fugue of thoughts, 'moments of being', and wrote one of her most extraordinary, symbolic essays about the death of a moth. Woolf pondered the existence of a female sentence. If there is one, she is one of its architects, and her style the first point of orientation for considering the possibility today. There *is* a Woolfian sentence. Is there, by analogy, a female mark? If so, it arises from multiple factors,

109

temporal, historical, social, as well as physical and psychological, but one of them stems from a community of precursors, and what they did. The conversation is live between Mary Cassatt, Gwen John, Marie Laurencin, Elizabeth Blackadder, Prunella Clough, Louise Bourgeois and their successors. But this question about art and gender is huge. And many young contemporary artists are redefining responses to the issue through their art, their approach, their individual touch.

A park is a work in itself, Sarah told me, somewhat like a painting, somewhere we go to play, an unreal place, a metaphor of creativity. Regent's Park was an innovation when it was first made for a city where thousands of people are all crowded together, but where, if so desired, each of them can enjoy solitude. In Sarah's pantheon each woman appears as an artist must: she is a solitary, but she dwells in the extended room of one's own that is this in-between place, the urban park.

Sarah uses large brushes, some as broad as brooms, as well as very fine, tiny ones – no doubt a single hair of a goat or some such refinement. She also

has a battery of aerosols in every colour – and with them she elicits fleeting, subtle epiphanies moving over the smooth non-absorbent aluminium plane of her pictures: here a flurry of notes, there a sudden vivid illuminated miniature of a duck, or a moth.

But it is not only the colours, or the light and motion of the paint, that make Sarah Pickstone's studio a different world from the one I left when she opened her door.

We also talked about painting and time. A park is a place where time changes rhythm, and you can take your time. Sarah has made images of the seasons and speaks of painting as 'being in the moment', 'making time happen', and of 'a child-like obsession with making your own time'. A park is an enclave where time opens up a funnel into another kind of time; 'opening' is an image that Sarah likes – as action and as revelation. A painting is like a novel or a poem in that it institutes another time: it overcomes the conditions of stillness and two-dimensionality, to carry us through time to see…the flicker of light in diaphanous willow fronds or the misty water in a fountain; Elizabeth Barrett

Hylas study, 2009

Browning stealing mistletoe or Plath typing away.

The philosopher Eugenio Trias, who sadly died in February 2013, writes about how the word for time in Latin, *tempus*, comes from the same root as the word for temple.[1] Sacred spaces are places where time is ordered differently.

By connecting Sarah's painting to theories of sacred space and time, I do not mean to attribute to it any religious or spiritual meanings in a literal way, but rather to propose that the way she illuminates her themes transports us into another dimension of time, which can be felt and experienced through the touch of the paint itself, the vitality of the colours. This experience is what the crowds who visit the National Gallery, Tate Modern, Tate St Ives, the New Walsall Art Gallery, Nottingham Contemporary or Roche Court are looking for from art, at least in part. They have plenty of other reasons, too, of course. But solitude in the midst of assembly, transit to another place (temporary but with lasting transformational effects perhaps) can be the gifts an artist makes to us. It is painting that shows us how

to look: it is more interesting to look at apples after seeing Cézanne's, a different experience of brown furniture after Doris Salcedo's monumental salvaged piles of it. Sarah Pickstone remarked how dazzlingly Manet paints the rose on the bar at the Folies Bergère, and said how she, too, loves to paint roses; she has transposed this richly symbolic flower into a tribute to the writer Fanny Burney – portraying her as a full-blown orange rose, rich in stamens.

Artists can reconfigure our vision from the inside, and colour above all needs artists to be revealed: the sixteenth-century painter Federico Barocci was a revelation when his work was brought from Urbino to the National Gallery, London in 2013. His delicate, glowing and fluid fabrics and flesh can also be felt vibrating in Sarah Pickstone's own absorption in textiles, in plumage, in a single moth's complicated, variegated shades and patterned wings. How long did it take for us to realise that the air itself is coloured? That shadows can be prismatic? Newton knew it, but it took the Impressionists to make us see it. The writer

1. Eugenio Trias, 'Thinking Religion: The Symbol and the Sacred', in *Religion*, eds. Jacques Derrida and Gianni Vattimo (Cambridge: Polity Press, 1998), pp. 95–110:110, quoting Ernst Cassirer, *The Philosophy of Symbolic Forms* (1955), Vol. 2. See also my letter in *London Review of Books*, Vol. 34. No.12, 30 August 2012.

Annie Dillard says that by dint of intensive daily looking at the creek by her house, she 'learned to recognise, slowing down, the difference in texture of the light reflected from mud bank, water, grass, or frog'.[2]

Most of us can't do that without painters; we need them to show us how.

When I left Sarah Pickstone's studio I thought of Lily Briscoe at the end of *To the Lighthouse*:

Quickly, as if she were recalled by something over there, she turned to her canvas. There it was – her picture. Yes, with all its greens and blues, its lines running up and across, its attempt at something. It would be hung in the attics, she thought; it would be destroyed. But what did that matter? she asked herself, taking up her brush again. She looked at the steps; they were empty; she looked at her canvas; it was blurred. With a sudden intensity, as if she saw it clear for a second, she drew a line there, in the centre. It was done; it was finished. Yes, she thought, laying down her brush in extreme fatigue, I have had my vision.[3]

Virginia Woolf is reflecting on herself and her own dream of writing, and anticipating possible disappointments as well as triumphs, and in writing this marvellous ending to her novel, she issues a lasting manifesto for why artists make their art.

113

Lake trees, 2009

2. Annie Dillard, *Pilgrim at Tinker Creek*, 1969.
3. Virginia Woolf, *To the Lighthouse*, 1927.

Studio, London

Acknowledgements

Thank you to Laura Macaulay, publisher at Daunt
Books for making this book possible. Huge thanks
too to the excellent Daunt Books team: Karen Maine,
editor, Emily Rhodes who first saw the work at
The New Art Centre and to Alice Laurent the
book's designer.

There are many friends and colleagues who have
helped. Thank you to:

Martin Mills, Elizabeth West, Charles Pickstone,
Dorothee Gillessen, Guy Martin, Karen Holden,
Cathy Bor, Sophie Pelham, Beate Mjaaland, Frances
Spalding, Fay Ballard, Fiona Parashar, Claire Lewis,
Dermot Coleman, Madeleine Bessborough, Stephen
Feeke, Claire Lilley, Frances Barry, Emily Jones,
Sandra Penketh, Angela Semata, Anne Ryan, Liz
Irwin, Gabrielle Tregear, Kate Bates, Meike
Ziervogel, Sheila Lawson, Valerie Scott, Lucy Neill,
Tracy Bohan and Philip Watson.

Thank you to all the contributors who generously
gave, lent or made work for the book and thank you
to Laura Braun who also photographed the art work.

Thank you to Ali Smith and to Marina Warner.

Text and Illustration Acknowledgements

Text Permissions

Page 23: 'On the Difficulty of Conjuring up a Dryad', Sylvia Plath, *Collected Poems*. Reprinted with the permission of Faber and Faber Ltd.

Page 29: Extract from 'Tears, Idle Tears' by Elizabeth Bowen. Reproduced with permission of Curtis Brown Group Ltd, London, on behalf of the estate of Elizabeth Bowen. Copyright © Elizabeth Bowen 1941.

Page 40: Extracts from *Katherine Mansfield Notebooks: Complete Edition*, edited by Margaret Scott, University of Minnesota Press, 2002.

Page 45: 'The Death of the Moth', Virginia Woolf, *The Death of the Moth And Other Essays*, The Hogarth Press, 1942.

Page 58: Extract from *Flush: A Biography*, Virginia Woolf, The Hogarth Press, 1933.

Page 74: Extract from *Frankenstein; or, The Modern Prometheus*, Mary Shelley, first published by Lackington, Hughes, Harding, Mavor & Jones, 1818.

Page 79: Extract from 'The Apprentice Years: 35', Frances Burney, *Frances Burney Journals and Letters*, Penguin Books, 2001. Copyright © Peter Sabor and Lars E. Troide, 2001.

Image credits

Page 3: *Playbill, Broadway and Futura*, Fiona Banner, 2002. Full Stops: Steel, paint. Courtesy the artist and Frith Street Gallery London.

Page 21: 'Not Waving But Drowning' poem and drawing, Stevie Smith, *Collected Poems*. Reprinted with the permission of Faber and Faber Ltd.

Page 25: 'Willow near Grantchester', Sylvia Plath, *Sylvia Plath: Drawings*, ed. Frieda Hughes. Reprinted with the permission of Faber and Faber Ltd.

Page 28: 'Sylvia Plath interviewing Elizabeth Bowen for *Mademoiselle*', May 1953, Mortimer Rare Book Room, Smith College. Copyright © Black Star. Reprinted with the permission of Smith College.

Page 41: *Fig Leaf Blood* photograph by Patti Smith. Reprinted with the permission of Patti Smith.

Page 46: Front cover of *The Death of the Moth And Other Essays* by Virginia Woolf, Hogarth Press, August, 1942. Jacket illustration and design by Vanessa Bell. Copyright © Estate of Vanessa Bell. Courtesy Henrietta Garnett.

Page 59: Front cover of *Flush: A Biography* by Virginia Woolf, published by The Hogarth Press, 1933. Used by permission of The Random House Group Limited.

Page 60: *Self-portrait as a Rubbish Bin*, Michael Landy, 2012. Courtesy the artist and Thomas Dane Gallery, London.

Page 66: *Aurora Leigh: A Poem in Nine Books*, Elizabeth Barrett Browning, Smith, Elder & Co., 1898.

Page 71: Stephen Gill, extract from *Pigeons*, to be published by Nobody in 2014. Copyright © Stephen Gill.

Page 80: Front cover *Evelina, or, The History of a Young Lady's Entrance into the World* by Fanny Burney, Macmillan and Co Ltd, 1903. Cover illustration by Hugh Thomson.

Page 82: *Mask XIII*, John Stezaker, 2006. Tate Collection. Image courtesy of The Approach, London.

Page 88: *Oak Tree*. Courtesy Laura Braun.

Page 90: *Middlemarch: A Study of Provincial Life* by George Eliot, Vol. 1, First edition, William Blackwood and Sons, 1871.

Page 104: *Wise Children* by Angela Carter. Copyright © The British Library Board, Add 88891/1/16, f.1.

Page 108: Cover of *Oeuvres Poétiques d'Arthur Rimbaud*, Copyright © 1964 Garnier Flammarion Paris, portrait of Rimbaud by Ernest Delahaye, 1875.

Page 114: 'Studio, London' Courtesy Miki Slingsby.

Work by Sarah Pickstone

Page 4: *Park 2*, 2004. Oil and acrylic on canvas. 264x206 cm. Courtesy Saatchi Gallery.

Page 6: *Elizabeth Barrett Browning Steals Mistletoe*, 2010. Oil and acrylic on panel, 72x58 cm. Courtesy Catherine Vlasto.

Page 11: *Willow*, 2011. Watercolour on paper, 51x36 cm. Private collection.

Page 16: *Stevie Smith and the Willow*, 2011. Oil and acrylic on aluminium panel, 230x200 cm. Courtesy National Museums Liverpool, Walker Art Gallery.

Page 20: *Love is Everything, One Looks for It*, 2013. Oil and acrylic on panel, 142x122 cm. Courtesy Yomi Rodrig.

Page 22: *Sylvia*, 2010. Oil and acrylic on canvas, 230x200 cm. Courtesy Jill Hackel and Andrzej Zarzycki Collection.

Page 26: *Sylvia Googled*, 2010. Watercolour on paper, 51x36 cm. Courtesy Mercer Art Gallery, Harrogate Borough Council.

Page 27: *Plath Winged*, 2010. Watercolour on paper, 31x23 cm. Courtesy Mercer Art Gallery, Harrogate Borough Council.

Page 31: *Bowen Smokes*, 2010. Watercolour and pigment on paper, 51x36 cm. Courtesy Mercer Art Gallery, Harrogate Borough Council.

Page 38: *Red Underwing*, 2010. Oil and acrylic on panel, 72x58 cm. Courtesy Mercer Art Gallery, Harrogate Borough Council.

Page 44: *Woolf*, 2010. Oil and acrylic on panel, 72x58 cm. Courtesy Karen and Mark Smith.

Page 50: *Orlando*, 2013.Oil and acrylic on panel, 72x58 cm. Courtesy Judy Weston.

Page 52: *Woolf Googled*, 2010. Watercolour on paper, 28x22 cm. Courtesy Marina Warner.

Page 57: *Orlando drawing*, 2013. Acrylic and watercolour on paper, 51x36 cm. Courtesy New Art Centre, Salisbury.

Page 63: *Ebb and BT*, 2009. Watercolour on paper, 31x23 cm. Courtesy Ali Smith.

Page 65: *Aurora Leigh*, 2007. Watercolour, 46x30 cm. Courtesy Christine Chang Hanway.

Page 75: *Gesture*, 2007. Oil and acrylic on canvas, 270x240 cm. Courtesy Kukje Gallery, Seoul.

Page 78: *The Poet*, 2008. Oil and acrylic on canvas, 120x100 cm. Private collection.

Page 85: *Gibbous Moon*, 2007. Oil and acrylic on canvas, 270x240 cm. Courtesy Kukje Gallery, Seoul.

Page 87: *Moth*, 2010. Watercolour on paper, 15x11 cm. Courtesy Ali Smith.

Page 89: *Eliot*, 2011. Oil and acrylic on panel, 142x122 cm. Courtesy Kate and Micheal Bates.

Page 92: *Triton*, 2006. Acrylic on canvas, 50x38 cm. Courtesy Sheila Lawson.

Page 99: *Crimson Leaf*, 2011. Acrylic on canvas, 38x30 cm. Courtesy Carolyn and Tony Sceales.

Page 103: *Fountain girls*, 2006. Watercolour on paper, 40x30 cm. Courtesy John Cavanagh.

Page 106: *Park 5*, 2004. 320x230 cm. Courtesy Saatchi Gallery.

Page 111: *Hylas study*, 2009. Watercolour on paper, 46x30 cm. Courtesy

Jill Hackel and Andrzej Zarzycki.

Courtesy of the artist

Page viii: *Neo Classik*, 2006. Oil and acrylic on canvas. 320x230 cm.

Page 15: *Bed*, 2004. Pencil on paper. 31x23 cm.

Page 35: *Plane*, 2001. Pencil on paper. 31x23 cm.

Page 37: *Katherine Mansfield's Moth*, 2011. Oil and acrylic on panel. 230x200 cm.

Page 43: *Mansfield Googled*, 2011. Oil on panel. 72x58 cm.

Page 49: *Moth*. Photo. 2013.

Page 55: *Up Here*, 2003. Oil on canvas. 30x22 cm.

Page 56: *Woolf Thinking*, 2010. Watercolour. 31x23 cm.

Page 67: *The Vision of Aurora Leigh*, 2007. Oil and acrylic on canvas. 32x24 cm.

Page 68: *Birds*, 2004. Watercolour on paper. 41x30 cm.

Page 76: *Shelley*, 2013. Oil and acrylic on aluminium panel. 230x200 cm.

Page 81: *Fanny Burney Thinks Her Hat into a Rose*, 2013. Oil and acrylic on panel. 72x58 cm.

Page 97: *Park*. Photo.

Page 105: *Can't Give You Anything But Love*, 2013. Oil and acrylic on aluminium panel. 230x200 cm.

Page 113: *Lake Trees*, 2009. Watercolour detail.

Every reasonable effort has been made to trace copyright holders, but if there are any errors or omissions, Daunt Books will be pleased to insert the appropriate acknowledgment in any subsequent edition.

Contributor List

Fiona Banner is visual artist. Her work centres on the problems and possibilities of language, both written and metaphorical. She is based in London.

Laura Braun is a photographer living and working in London.

Amanda Coe is a screenwriter and novelist. Her second novel *Getting Colder*, is published by Virago in November 2014.

Lara Feigel is a lecturer in English at King's College London and the author of *The Love-charm of Bombs: Restless Lives in the Second World War* and *Literature, Cinema, Politics: Reading between the Frames*.

Stephen Gill's photographs have been exhibited at many international galleries and museums including London's National Portrait Gallery. Publications of his East London photographic studies include *Hackney Wick*, *Archaeology in Reverse*, and *Buried*.

Paul Hobson is the Director of Modern Art Oxford. He joined the gallery in August 2013, following six years as Director of the Contemporary Art Society and former senior roles at the Showroom Gallery, Serpentine Gallery, and Royal Academy of Arts, London.

Jackie Kay's most recent books are *Red Dust Road*, *Fiere*, and *Reality, Reality*. She is Professor of Creative Writing at Newcastle University.

Olivia Laing is the author of *To the River* and *The Trip to Echo Spring*. She's currently working on *The Lonely City*, a book about urban loneliness.

Michael Landy lives and works in London. He is best known for his 2001 installation, *Break Down*, where he catalogued and then destroyed all of his possessions. Most recently, he was associate artist of the National Gallery.

Emily Rhodes is a writer, blogger, bookseller, and the inventor of Emily's Walking Book Club. She contributes to *The Spectator* and has just finished writing her first novel.

Iain Sinclair has lived in East London for more than forty years, from where he has launched the expeditions that have fuelled books that include *London Orbital*, *Hackney, That Rose-Red Empire*, and *Lights Out for the Territory*.

John Stezaker uses photographs and printed material to create collages involving various interventions such as excisions, maskings, cuts, rotations, and visual concordances. Recent solo exhibitions of his work have been held in London, Tel Aviv, Berlin, and Luxembourg.

Ali Smith is a writer of novels, short stories, plays, and criticism. She lives in Cambridge.

Craig Taylor is the author of three books, including *Londoners: The Days and Nights of London Now – As Told by Those Who Love It, Hate It, Live It, Left It, and Long for It*. He is the editor of the literary magazine, *Five Dials*.

Marina Warner is a writer of fiction, cultural history, and criticism. Her collected essays on art and artists, *The Symbol Gives Rise to Thought*, will appear in two volumes next year, from Violette Editions.